CW00471226

The Saturn/Pluto Phenomenon

THE
SATURN
PLUTO
PHENOMENON

by
Joy Michaud & Karen Hilverson

SAMUEL WEISER, INC.
York Beach, Maine

First published in 1993 by
Samuel Weiser, Inc.
Box 612
York Beach, ME 03910

Copyright © 1993 Joy Michaud and Karen Hilverson
All rights reserved. No part of this publication may be reproduced or
transmitted in any form or by any means, electronic or mechanical, including photocopy, without permission in writing from Samuel Weiser, Inc.
Reviewers may quote brief passages.

Library of Congress Cataloging-in-Publication Data

Michaud, Joy, 1944-
    The Saturn-Pluto phenomenon / by Joy Michaud & Karen Hilverson.
        p.   cm.
    Includes bibliographical references.
        1. Saturn (Planet)—Miscellanea.   2. Pluto (Planet)—Miscellanea.
    3. Astrology—Miscellanea.   I. Hilverson, Karen, 1950-
    II. Title.
    BF1724.2.S3M53   1993
    133.5'3—dc20   91-35566
                                                                     CIP
ISBN 0-87728-722-8
BJ

Excerpts from "The Wasteland" in *Collected Poems 1909-1962* by T.S. Eliot, copyright © 1936
Harcourt Brace Jovanovich, Inc., copyright © 1964,1963 T.S. Eliot, reprinted by permission of
the publisher. Permission also granted by Faber and Faber Ltd., publisher of the work in the
United Kingdom.

Excerpts from "East Coker" in *Four Quartets*, copyright © 1943 T.S. Eliot and renewed in 1971 by
Esme Valerie Eliot, reprinted by permission of Harcourt Brace Jovanovich, Inc. Permission also
granted by Faber and Faber Ltd., publisher of the work in the United Kingdom.

Cover illustration, entitled "Saturn," and illustrations within the text are
copyright © 1993 Erich Holmann.   Used by kind permission of the artist.

The charts in this book were calculated and printed by Astrolabe, Inc. of
Brewster, MA, using its *Nova* and *Printwheels* computer programs.

Printed in the United States of America

The paper used in this publication meets the minimum requirements of the
American National Standard for Permanence of Paper for Printed Library
Materials Z39.48-1984.

Contents

Preface

During our life on earth, the influence from the planet Saturn is of great importance. Saturn is the key to the whole chart, and no knowledge of self can truly be obtained without first recognizing the influence, as well as the limitations, that this planet imposes on our human condition. Within theological symbolism, Saturn is God the Father or the Jehovah of Moses and the Old Testament, and is emblematic of the living image of God.[1]

Saturn represents structure, and structure as we know is an essential part of the human experience. Structure consists of many things—conformities, time, form, order and organization are just a few of its many components. Saturn's position in a birth chart indicates the area where structure is necessary within that life and points to an area of required learning and responsibility. Until the lesson implied by Saturn is understood, limitation, restriction, even suffering can often be the result. This may be connected to personality, values, learning and communication, emotions, parents and home, children, love and affections, work or health, partnerships, relationships with others, sex, death, the search for higher knowledge, success or place in the world, figures of authority, friendships, confinement even psychic influences—the list is long.

The structure given by Saturn is a necessary requisite in the formation of the personality, and thus, it should be seen as a force for good when properly understood. As soon as we accept responsibility on an inner level for our own limitations, fears, and sometimes failures (which may manifest through or because of the apparent limited structure of our own personal world) without blaming others or circumstances, then real growth and the beginning of true understanding can begin. From the greater self-awareness

---

[1] See Blavatsky's *The Secret Doctrine* (Pasadena, CA: Theosophical University Press, 1971), p.334.

that develops when working with Saturn, there comes the ability to work more consciously with other planetary elements within the psyche, as well as with a combination of these influences, such as sub-personalities.

Esoteric astrology recognizes that Saturn is the key or pivot, in regard to all the other planets. To work with any planetary influence on an inner level—that is to say, to understand and integrate their influence more wholly into a conscious action, rather than an unconscious reaction—one must first understand and work with the disciplines and lessons associated with Saturn. For instance, Pluto can open up great channels of transformation which can also lead to the greatest creativity, but without help from Saturn, balance is hard to achieve. Neptune can lead to divine love free from illusion, but without the stabilization from Saturn, this cannot even start to be attained. Uranus, although in mythology the father of Saturn, again cannot ever be truly actualized into reality until Saturn's message is integrated and accepted. This system of order that Saturn represents within the universe has been recognized by many astrologers and philosophers down through the ages.

In this book, Pluto is also discussed. Saturn and Pluto are both Lords of Karma, both reapers of souls, and both are hard task masters. However, where Saturn supplies the necessary lessons, Pluto's task seems to be to bring to the surface the past effects of a person's actions and conduct during the successive phases of his existence. Some of this karmic residue may represent certain parts within our natures that we choose to ignore. It is perhaps for this reason alone that certain transits or progressions from Pluto may be experienced as exceedingly devastating and destructive.

Pluto is a generation planet as it stays in one sign for several years, and it has influence over mass consciousness and racial memory. Therefore, as men or women symbolically experience death and rebirth within their personal lives, each generation and race will go through the same transforming process. At this time,[2] Pluto is in its own sign of Scorpio, and already we are experiencing much darkness and despair within our world— mass starvation, often through mass aggression, caused by those who wield the more powerful weapons of destruction, as well as terrible devastation of the planet as a whole.

---

[2] Pluto is in Scorpio from November 1983 until November 1995.

The image of Pluto has rarely been positive. Often he will represent certain things we may turn away from, such as thoughts of death and other dark and hidden elements of the unconscious. Perhaps we should perceive that something as dark and fearsome as Pluto also has an opposite side, equal in its creative willpower and genius, and encompasses love realized through occult awareness and initiation.[3]

Where balance from Saturn does not exist within the personality, Pluto's force may often be unscrupulous, bent on domination and the exploitation and suppression of the weakest parts of the whole. This may occur through power games experienced within personal relationships, the family, or society, but also exists as a dominant and controlling force within the individual personality, blocking any conversion from taking place. Where balance from Saturn does exist, Pluto can begin to help identify and determine the struggle between the ego self and the soul self, and so will start to initiate a channel towards immortality.

—Joy Michaud

---

[3] Initiation here refers to the mysteries of life, as well as the mysteries of death and rebirth.

Introduction

A few years ago, I worked in a clinic for alternative medicine. We saw people suffering from many complaints, physical and mental, and while working there I started to wonder why some patients responded to therapy and others didn't, why some recovered from such crippling illnesses as arthritis while others found no relief. Some people rid themselves of tumors and growths; others with the same disease didn't. There were patients that had remission from MS and other muscular-based diseases, and many who did not improve at all. Some people attending the clinic suffered from various forms of neurosis, and after therapy and counseling, became more able to cope with their various problems, while others stayed the same or even became worse.

"Why," I asked, "do some improve, while others, however hard we try with them, do not?" It became increasingly clear that patients' illnesses were in some way connected with their own minds and were brought about, to a certain extent, by their own repressed thought patterns.

After working in the clinic for 18 months, I decided to leave and study psychology, in order to learn more about how the human mind works. I took a two-year course in psychotherapy and hypnotherapy, after which I qualified and started practicing privately.

As time went on, I continued to expand my knowledge of the mind by attending various schools of psychological thought, as well as reading many books. Roberto Assagioli's *Psychosynthesis*[1] impressed me very much. What I was looking for was a way of working with people on an inner level, so that they could develop as individuals, rather than according to any set guidelines or rules. I wanted to encourage clients to develop their own

---

[1] Roberto Assagioli, *Psychosynthesis* (New York: Penguin, 1971).

individuality and to show them how to turn weaknesses into strengths. In other words, I wanted to enable them to become responsible for themselves, rather than blame others or their circumstances for their health or state of mind. This seemed important.

At this time, while learning about and working with transpersonal psychology, I began to use the idea of subpersonalities with patients. In this theory, we all have several different personalities within our individual psyches, but often these are alienated rather than united. For example: imagine four main subpersonalities within the person known as Joan Smith. (See figure 1 on page 3.)

1) The homemaker—kind, caring, likes security, enjoys entertaining;

2) The friend—enjoys others' company, open and loyal;

3) The philosopher—enjoys sharing ideas with others, interested in many subjects, likes traveling, optimistic and open;

[Up to now everything is fine, but let's add the fourth subpersonality.]

4) The victim—anxiety from childhood, feels dumb, daft, self-conscious, lacks confidence, isolated as a teenager.

[Immediately you can see how this fourth subpersonality, if allowed to get out of proportion, can take all the energy from the other three.]

While working on my own subpersonalities, I discovered "Rosie" within myself. She was interested in nature, and all things connected to nature, be it herbs and their properties, healing energies, or astrology. She was a part of myself I had denied expression to while working as a psychotherapist. This was possibly why I never felt entirely complete in my work and was always searching for that elusive something I could never find. Now I needed to let Rosie develop, and I took a course in astrological counseling and brought this into my work as a psychotherapist.

Presently everything made sense. I explained to patients why I believed we all experienced confusion, struggles, pain, and sorrow, but that we needed to understand and work with these perplexities rather than ignore them as though they didn't exist. This only brought neurosis and a diminished ability to function as a whole person, affecting us mentally or physically and sometimes both. I illustrated how, when we were born, it

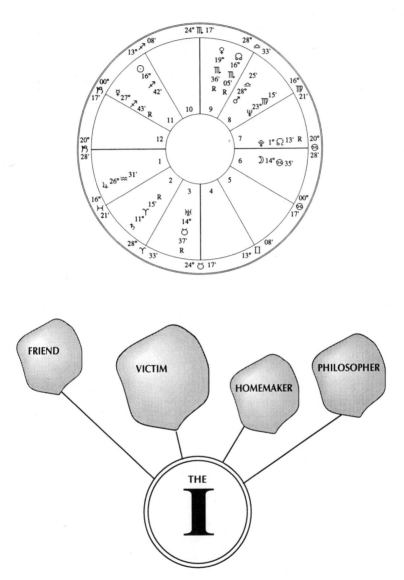

Figure 1. Four subpersonalities are indicated in Joan Smith's natal chart. Birth data has been withheld for confidentiality. Chart has been calculated with Placidus Houses, using Nova/Printwheels.

was as though a clock started ticking, and that certain planetary emana-
tions—or energies from the planets—played on that inner clock bringing
cycles of learning into our lives. All we experienced came from within.
Even medical science acknowledged that a large number of illnesses were
psychosomatic—I explained how these planetary energies were not sent by
some wicked god who wanted to hurt us, but were there to teach us
something. It seemed logical, therefore, that if we learned to work with
these energies consciously and understood what they were trying to teach
us, life would at last begin to make sense. We would have more peace of
mind and freedom of thought.

I was now running various courses and seminars on psychology and
astrology, and was asked to do a one day workshop combining the two. This
was when the notion of working directly with a planetary energy rather than
through a subpersonality emerged. I was experiencing a Saturn opposition
to my sun sign at that time, so I chose to work with Saturn, although I did
not initially recognize his great importance. The problem I wanted Saturn
to help me with was two-fold: the only way I could cope with my extreme
sensitivity in certain situations, was to cover up with a show of power. For
example, if giving a talk to a group, be there three people or 300, I would
appear confident and successful, but, deep inside me there was a feeling of
deep dissatisfaction. I was hiding the real me through fear, and used (or
rather was used by) a show of false power and strength. So the question I
wanted to ask Saturn was: "How can I use power in the right way?" I
recorded the following meditation.

> On the inner journey I reached the mountains. They were very
> much like Mount Athos; their huge crags towered above me.
> There was a chain nailed into the rocks with which I pulled
> myself up. Mostly the way was very steep. I reached the plateau
> and saw a vast temple rising out of the mist. When the gatekeep-
> er opened the massive door, I saw that he was a centurion. He
> seemed very powerful and slightly intimidating. I told him why
> I was there, and he let me in. Inside the hall there were many
> people, most of whom I could not see properly as they were in
> deep shadows. Those I could see were dressed in aristocratic
> medieval costumes, and appeared very clever and superior. My

Saturn is in Gemini in the 7th opposing the Ascendant. I felt small, insignificant and inferior. I kept trying to make myself larger but to little avail, as I kept shrinking. I walked down the hall experiencing an increased feeling of inadequacy. Approaching Saturn, I knew that I had been here before. He was dressed in a white robe, had long white hair and beard, and very dark, kind, but piercing eyes, and he sat on a white marble throne. At one point I had to give him a gift. I stretched out my closed hand to him, and as it opened, a butterfly sat there. (This was a spontaneous response from my unconscious, and at the time I had no idea of its meaning. In fact I forgot all about it when I wrote down my notes.) He seemed pleased and took the gift.

I asked him, "I have come to learn how to use power in the right way."

He replied, "Use it only with great responsibility and compassion," and he held out his hand to me and smiled.

I stepped out of myself and became the god sitting on his throne. I looked down on my subjects, seeing them not through the eyes of fear or power, but through the eyes of kindness and compassion. In front of me was the whole spectrum of humanity, struggling like Joy to make some sense of it all. Some were aristocratic, some humble; some had plenty, others nothing. Some were clever, others had little education, some had talents connected to music and the arts, some had little meaning in their lives. Some appeared ill, others were lost, lonely and sad. My heart went out to them all in loving kindness. I looked down on Joy, she was very small, I picked her up, and stood her by me. She grew as large as myself—I then sat her on the arm of the throne. She seemed very happy.

I stepped out of Saturn and became Joy again. Saturn said, "You must never compare yourself with others. All are different and unique. Look beyond appearances. The planetary energies play on the mirror of your mind and are thus projected out onto events, people, and objects in the outer world. This looks like reality to you, but it is only an illusion, as you only ever see the situation through your own mirror. If you understand this you have made the first step in understanding yourself and others. You have an intellectual understanding of how this works, but you can never perceive spiritual truths through the intellect alone. The true understanding of this is my gift to you; use it well."

I thanked him for his help, gratefully realizing that I was able to go back to him at any time. I said goodbye and took my leave. As I reached the door I saw that the gatekeeper had changed to a young fair-haired man dressed in white. He seemed kind and gentle as he let me out.

After writing up some notes, I experienced a quiet sense of peace and oneness with all. I looked out the window. The Sun was shining. Suddenly, a butterfly flew against the window and reminded me of my gift to Saturn, something I had forgotten when writing my notes. To me it seemed to represent the part of my mind that wanted to stay childish, that didn't want to grow up and face responsibility. Unconsciously, this was my gift to Saturn. In return he had offered me the true understanding of responsibility and strength. I felt very pleased with the bargain made.

• • •

I used the Saturn Meditation at the workshop with very promising results and decided to bring it into my practice. It did open up an entirely new dimension—I had found no single item before of such value in connection to my work, and yet it was very safe and extremely simple. Most patients responded well, saying, "Why didn't I know about this before? It would have made my life so much easier." They were all encouraged to use the tape at home to help them in any decision or difficulty they had to face. I saw people who had spent years trying to gain strength and independence, become strong and sure of themselves. I could not, of course, use this type of exercise on patients suffering any degree of psychosis! Their help must come through other means. The only people who did not respond were those who demanded that life should give them this or that, and who refused to take any responsibility for what happened to them. Some of this type— if patience was exercised, and it might mean waiting weeks or even months for the initial idea to be accepted—would start to respond when they realized the significance of the exercise, which is freedom from fear and limitation.

I started giving talks to astrology groups on the significance of working with Saturn and was pleased by the interest they created. I also gave more seminars and workshops specifically using the Saturn Meditation. I had feedback of a very positive nature. It seemed that as soon as people assumed their own responsibilities, much inner growth took place. The effect was also beneficial with certain physical complaints.

I wondered if one could use the same type of meditation with the other planets, and tried to define some way of working with them, but to no avail. It seemed that Saturn was the balance for all the other planets, and in researching this theory, I found that certain esoteric writers and astrologers, such as Alan Leo, Alice Bailey, and Madame Blavatsky, confirmed this theory. Pluto, however, did seem to be the exception. How to work with him, I was not sure. I tried for several months to find a similar meditation for Pluto, but it was not until I had a Pluto opposing Mercury transit, that I discovered how to go into the underworld to meet the god there. I was very nervous but chose to go. The whole experience was very enlightening. When shown my darker side, I was told by Pluto, "Do not be frightened of what to you looks like evil, it is only goodness untransformed."

I chose not to work with any of it then but to come back again when I felt I was ready, which I did. The effect of working with Pluto was very beneficial, but in a different way to Saturn. Afterwards, when I discussed my experience with a friend, she made the remark, "I have worked on certain problems for years, and although I have received benefits from this, I have never felt I've really let go of them." It seems, therefore, that when we have worked through certain difficulties regarding responsibility to ourselves and others, we are ready to transform these energies with the help of Pluto.

Saturn limits our conscious mind and causes restrictions and difficulties in the physical world—whereas, Pluto, the outermost planet of the solar system, limits our unconscious mind and restricts us on the inner levels of discovery and growth. Examples of this are people who have a mission, particularly of an idealistic nature, but who have a hard aspect from Pluto to contend with. These people are often motivated by a need for power rather than altruism. This is not to say that the motivation is not sincere, but unconscious forces over which they have no control are driving them and continue to do so until they accept and recognize these as their own. Often they will deny any need to understand themselves on an inner level, and there may be a deep fear of the unconscious, and of losing control.

Some people working through a Pluto aspect may have an intellectual knowledge of psychology and may even work as counselors, social workers, or in a similar profession. In the extreme, they invariably ignore others' opinions or codes, exert power over others in some form or other, and are always "right." If on a spiritual path they will choose to jump from kindergarten to university, without working through what is in between. In the most extreme cases, they are almost entirely possessed by Pluto's power. Until they accept responsibility regarding their conscious and unconscious actions, the energy of Pluto will use this person mercilessly. But unless they realize this, they have no choice in anything, be it their own health, relations with others, or any other facet of their lives. As they control others, so the unconscious energy of Pluto controls them in an endless dance of death, until the time comes when they realize this unconscious process of control. But this awareness does not always come easily, as Pluto's power comes from such a deep level and is often so completely unconscious, that they are unaware of its nature and existence. *They need to work first through the lessons of Saturn, before Pluto's great wealth can be realized.*

The Pluto Meditation is used less frequently than the one connected to Saturn. Because until certain responsibilities connected to Saturn are acknowledged and worked through, they cannot be transformed. These are not responsibilities connected to social morality or obligations laid down by society or the social group we call our own, but responsibility for our own actions on the deepest levels of being.

Do not be daunted by the task. See it rather as an act of happiness and love, a reaching out to wholeness. Remember, we all need to learn, at our own pace and in our own way, the particular lesson that is ours. All lessons are different, all are spun from past desires based on illusion as to the true meaning of life.

For those who are knowledgeable in astrology, I hope these ideas open up a new perspective. I also hope that readers with no understanding of the planetary influences will perhaps investigate further and gain some insight from reading about the experiences described. Certainly the meditations are not meant to be an anesthetic but are a positive step towards a better understanding of the self, and a help in solving problems which previously seemed to be without solution.

Part I

SATURN

Saturn delays, retards and hinders for no other purpose than
that perfection shall be reached by all things and all men. Saturn
concentrates and purifies until all impurities are as it were
precipitated to the bottom of each earth life, until right action
is performed *for right's sake only*.

————*Alan Leo*

Saturn in Mythology, Literature, and Art

The image of Saturn can be said to spring from time itself. His Greek name was Cronus (Time) and, as such, he was the force at the beginning and end of existence.[1] He was a legendary figure, a Titan—one of the elder gods produced by Earth and Heaven, who were themselves children of Chaos—or Kosmos—or space, which is the container of everything. Thus the ancient Greeks explained the process of creation. Saturn, it was said, devoured his own children, as time will devour all things on earth. However he did eventually disgorge his offspring who remained unscathed.

Similar creation stories can be traced to most of the ancient civilizations. The names may be different but the elements involved are the same: out of Chaos come Earth and Heaven who, in turn, produce a number of children, one of whom is a Saturn-like figure. It is as if a universal intuition has identified an important influence on human consciousness and reported it through tradition and legend for the generations to come. There is always the figure who destroys but also creates, and who brings forth new life from personal sacrifice.

The Saturnine temperament was traditionally sluggish and gloomy, known as "Melancholia." But Cornelius Agrippa of Nesheim remarked in his *De Occulta Philosophia 1509*[2] that the "Melancholy fury" stimulated the three highest human faculties: intellect, reasoning, and imagination. His observation was that a higher consciousness emerges from darkness.

This theory stimulated three of the greatest engravings by the medieval artist, Albrecht Dürer: "Melancholia," "St. Jerome," and "The Knight,

---

[1] Mythology taken from Bulfinch's *Age of Fable* (New York: Airmont Publishing Co., 1965).

[2] Cornelius Agrippa, *De Occulta Philosophia 1509*, cited in *Life and Times of Durer* by Adelaide Murgia (London: Hamlyn, 1970), p. 21.

Death and the Devil." They all incorporate the symbols of Saturn to communicate a basic teaching. In "St. Jerome," the old man has transformed his gloomy cell into an earthly paradise with Light streaming through the windows. He is busy studying, while his lion and hound lie down together. There is an hourglass above his head and a skull on the windowsill, but his writings emphasize industry and resolve rather than despondency. In "The Knight, Death and the Devil," resolve is once more the essence of the subject. The knight is riding through a wasteland accompanied by his faithful hound. He is followed by two eerie companions—Death with an hourglass and the Devil—but he rides diligently on, looking straight ahead. He is combating despondency with a sense of purpose. In "Melancholia," Dürer depicts a large angel carrying dividers, a clasped book and a large bunch of keys at his belt. There is a block of hewn granite, and a pair of scales. All about is the debris of a building site. A cherub is writing away, perched on a giant millwheel. Again, the symbolism is constructive rather than gloomy.

There are similar stories in medieval legends where the knights seek the Holy Grail and face many adversities in a cursed country—no more than a wasteland—to find the cup Christ used at the Last Supper, a cup which would restore the land to fertility and order. In modern times, the poet T. S. Eliot saw 20th century London in terms of a wasteland.

> *"Unreal City,*
> *Under the brown fog of a winter dawn,*
> *A crowd flowed over London Bridge, so many,*
> *I had not thought death had undone so many."* [3]

But unlike the medieval questers, Eliot's present-day characters never reach the Grail. Whether society beauty or barroom crone, all remain locked in their own private wilderness dreading the onset of old age and the coming of death. They remain waiting for rain in a parched land that offers little hope and even less comfort. In the Arthurian story, the knights cross the fearful, devastated landscape to reach a ruined castle. All around them they see death and destruction, but they persevere, and because of

---

[3] T.S. Eliot, "The Waste Land," lines 60-63, from *Collected Poems 1902-1962*, by T. S. Eliot (San Diego: Harcourt Brace Jovanovich, 1964 and London: Faber and Faber, Ltd., 1963).

their courage and determination, the Grail is revealed to them. Immediately the land is transformed into a beautiful country, and they are taught that the blighted appearance need only be transitory.

In the Saturn legends, elements of restriction, desolation, loneliness and despair disguise blessings—peace and joy somehow interweave. Heaven and hell are the same. This is the essential Saturn teaching as identified by some of the wisest. The human tendency to neglect the positive side of Saturn and remain in a state of isolation and despondency is only too obvious from Eliot's poem. The characters are full of fear and unanswered questions:

> *"My nerves are bad tonight. Yes, bad. Stay with me.*
> *"Speak to me. Why do you never speak. Speak.*
> *"What are you thinking of? What thinking? What?*
> *"I never know what you are thinking. Think."* [4]

Later, the lines are punctuated mercilessly with the repeated phrase: "HURRY UP PLEASE ITS TIME." Here is a form of hell on earth without respite or relief.

In *The Art of Synthesis*, Alan Leo comments:

> Saturn, as St. Peter, keeper of the keys of heaven and hell, guards the path leading upward and downward between the light and life immortal and the darkness and death of the mortal lower self. [5]

The Saturn energy is a gateway to the choice between restricted and unrestricted consciousness. Frequently, the Saturn experience is the two sides of the same coin: uncompromising demand to produce unlimited blessing.

The wisdom of the ancients perceived Saturn as a *reproach* rather than a curse. The Saturn influence must, of necessity, challenge human consciousness to question superficial social existence. The Saturn phenomenon is an indication of potential and a positive force in self-awareness. This is why Saturn rules the final card in the Tarot's major arcanum The World.

---

[4] T. S. Eliot, "The Waste Land," lines 111-114.

[5] Alan Leo, *The Art of Synthesis* (Rochester, VT: Inner Traditions, 1989), p. 92.

The World represents the ultimate in individual achievement. It is symbolized by a naked, dancing figure—a hermaphrodite. It is the dance of Shiva and of all initiates throughout time, and indicates that only through a spiritually directed movement can the world and the truth of existence truly be realized. The World dancer is a celebration of the Great Work accomplished. This is the potential offered to all seekers by the Saturn phenomenon.

How to Understand Saturn by Sign and House

To fully understand the influence of Saturn within the natal chart, all positions and aspects connected to this planet must be read individually. For example, it is necessary to look at the sign and house Saturn falls in, and the house Saturn rules or co-rules—although, of course, this is a secondary consideration and has slightly lesser significance but is still very important. If you look at your own chart now, using this simple procedure of Saturn in sign, house, and house ruled and/or co-ruled, you will immediately see the structure and confines of your own existence.[6] Then also look at each and every aspect Saturn makes to other planets. The complete synthesis of all this information is the message and the lesson that Saturn contains for you. The following simple examples show how people either project their Saturn on to others, or else allow their own energies to limit and restrict them, so they, in some way, end up prey to themselves. It happens to us all in some way and is generally more noticeable at times when we are affected by hard aspects from transits or progressions.

All the examples quoted are taken from case histories, and I hope they will give you some idea of what I want to convey. For instance, the placement of Saturn in Scorpio in the 12th ruling the 2nd means reading the sections on Saturn in Scorpio, the twelfth (Pisces) and the second (Taurus). The person with these placements initially felt a tremendous fear and persecution complex connected to a marriage that had ended. This lady was frightened that her ex-husband would take all her money. She seemed to have no control over her fears which had become quite obsessive. She also said she feared going mad. (Saturn in this chart formed part of a grand cross.)

---

[6] If you don't have your natal chart, see Appendix II, page 183, in order to pinpoint the sign Saturn falls in for you.

The house that Saturn rules or co-rules is important, and so are Saturn's aspects to other planets. For instance, hard aspects between Mars and Saturn are sure to cause difficulties, particularly in a male chart, as Mars is a masculine energy and Saturn will restrict it, often creating much anguish in connection to the person's masculine role and his ability to move ahead. Saturn in hard aspect to Venus will often give a sense of loss within relationships and will restrict the feminine principle, which can bring particular problems in a female's chart. One of the older interpretations of hard Venus-Saturn aspects is "sorrow in love." Saturn in hard aspect to the Moon will give a sense of emotional loss, and depression will occur at times within the particular emotional area concerned. Any hard aspect from Saturn to another planet will restrict that planet's energy, and until understood, it will cause difficulty and limitation. The following examples show how various Saturn placements worked for some of my clients.

Saturn exactly on the cusp between the 10th and 11th house in Taurus and ruling the 7th. This person married a friend from childhood who was wealthy. She said they did not get on from the start of the marriage; she complained he was weak and only ever thought of making money.

Saturn in Aquarius in the 4th and ruling the 3rd. A young lady who said, "I have given up all my friends and I have no interests since I started living with my boyfriend, he was the only friend I wanted. Now he wants his freedom and I have no one. I feel lonely, hurt and unwanted."

Saturn in Sagittarius in the 2nd and ruling the 3rd. He complained, "She restricts me in many ways by her possessiveness, she can never really understand me." There were also many difficulties over possessions and finance.

Saturn in Gemini conjunct the MC in the 10th and ruling the 5th, co-ruling the fourth. A person who had given up a great deal to get on in the world, who had achieved distinction and honor, but who said if he had a wish, it would be to have a really loving relationship with someone, as this was the only thing he had never had.

Saturn in Scorpio in the 9th house. The person concerned explained that she had separated from her husband through sexual difficulties caused through religion—the husband also came from a foreign culture.

So all other aspects connected to Saturn should be noted, as well as planets in the 10th house or conjuncting the MC. For as all these sensitive points are triggered by transit and progression so we are faced with situations that challenge us and force us to grow. To sit quietly and let life ride over us is not always the answer; the energy will still work itself out through other people or situations in our life. We then just become helpless victims. To work with and understand ourselves—if we possibly can—is the only satisfactory answer.

SATURN IN ARIES (OR THE 1ST HOUSE)

Saturn in Aries or the 1st house—ruling or co-ruling the 1st; conjuncting or in hard aspect to the ascendent; any hard aspects from Saturn to planets in the first.

There is often a lack of confidence, and a feeling of being restricted by others. For example, within marriage confidence may initially be obtained from the spouse, but as certain transits and progressions aspect Saturn, a strong feeling of restriction is often blamed on the partner or other people's attitudes. Inhibitions can cramp the whole personality. Feelings of responsibility may feel heavy, and occasionally there may be a need to avoid duty or avoid working through personal difficulties. Saturn in this position may cause a need for people to protect themselves and their own interests. Sometimes they will build a wall around themselves, which causes others' difficulty in interpreting their true motives. There is a deep need to prove themselves. Sometimes an inner fear motivates the need to come first. When this does not occur, depression can follow. More often than not there is a very poor self-image, as the Ascendant—and to a lesser extent the 1st house—is a lens through which the rest of the chart is projected. Thus this image of self is distorted—usually by feelings of inferiority—to the detriment of the rest of the nature and personality.

To learn what makes up their inner personality and who they really are is necessary for the growth of these individuals. Saturn is in its fall in Aries, and so it is important that these people get beyond self-imposed prisons to learn to work and share with others, on a one-to-one level of giving and receiving, but this can only come about when self-understanding leads to a better self-image. Until this happens, people with this position cannot learn to cooperate with others, and much unhappiness and fear is generated as they are always protecting themselves from imagined threats, which causes an endless need to guard self-interests. Self-reliance, self-understanding, and persistence should be aimed at. They need to truly learn to love and share with those they meet.

SATURN IN TAURUS (OR THE 2ND HOUSE)

Saturn in Taurus or the 2nd house—or ruling or co-ruling the 2nd; any planets in the 2nd in hard aspect to Saturn.

A deep lack of self-worth seems to accompany these positions. Sometimes these people choose a partner that triggers off this quality. Trouble through joint and individual possessions is common: money and other financial considerations become very important and are often a source of unhappiness. Often those who hold new age principles will deny this aspect of themselves and money or other objects will become a source of negativity as they try to reject this part in some way, and project its shadow side onto others. But the energy from this placement will make itself felt in other areas connected to possessions and values—and possessions cover a very wide field. The whole chart needs checking to find the area where this energy may manifest.

There is frequently a struggle connected to finance. This can in some cases lead to greed and a lack of generosity. With this position a person may own a great deal but have very little money actually in his or her pocket. There is usually a great burden connected to possessions—such as business worries, upkeep of properties, and dependency of others, such as employees, relatives, or parents. These individuals are often long-suffering, patient, and cautious—not to say stubborn at times, and often carry a deep fear that others only want them for what they own—hence the need to recognize their own worth by understanding where true values begin and false values end. This can only be achieved by their accepting human nature as it is, realizing they cannot get rid of it but can transform it and raise their values to a higher level.

SATURN IN GEMINI (OR THE 3RD HOUSE)

Saturn in Gemini or the 3rd house—or ruling or co-ruling the 3rd house; Saturn in hard aspect to any planet there in the 3rd.

Often there is a serious attitude to life, sometimes a limited education or the feeling that the education was less than adequate, causing these people to feel shy or awkward in intellectual situations. These people feel that they never know enough, although this may be hidden by an outer show. Speech may be impaired in some way, or there is difficulty with communication—the right word always just escaping at the wrong moment. This position can produce people who find it very difficult to communicate with others, or who over-compensate by talking too much. There may also be a feeling that others do not understand or share their own thoughts resulting in a feeling of alienation.

This placement can give intellectual ability if time and care is taken to develop these qualities. At best the mind is steady, impartial, and profound, but these qualities usually develop later in life and after much effort. Responsibility connected to speech and all communication, including the written word, is necessary before this is achieved. All aspects to Mercury need careful analysis in this respect. If we refuse this responsibility we may become our own victim and thus become very hardheaded and bitter. In recognizing that our mind and speech should be used as honestly and straightforwardly as possible, we gain much strength and start to think in terms of universal thought. We realize that our thoughts really do create our world—and that before we can even begin the search for "truth," we must become "truth."

SATURN IN CANCER (OR THE 4TH HOUSE)

Saturn in Cancer or the 4th house—or ruling or co-ruling the 4th house; or in hard aspect from Saturn to any planets there in the 4th.

The desire for security may assume large proportions at times. At certain periods the home life may feel unhappy or restricted in some way.

There may be sad incidents connected with the family, and great care and responsibility is needed in this respect. Often there is pessimism and suspicion of others—although others are usually needed to supply some emotional support. This can be a person who seems to drain others emotionally, or someone who is always looking for a degree of emotional satisfaction through others. Men may find this position of Saturn difficult, especially if emotions tend to be hidden. Sometimes emotional security may be sought through sexual involvement, or security is sought in some material object, such as a property or a collection of some kind, or there is just a need to acquire. The Moon's sign, house position, and aspects can be helpful in pinpointing where other areas of emotional hardship may occur.

There is often a loss of security in childhood, and people with this placement are programmed to find it in some way. What they do not realize is while they look for this fulfillment on a purely personal or material level, they will always lack the true gratification they seek. By taking full responsibility for their emotional make-up—without blaming others, particularly the parents—they realize the message that the soul requires them to learn. This is often difficult to do, but until they investigate and accept their own personal world of feeling, their security is forever threatened, and the lesson they need to learn goes unheeded.

SATURN IN LEO (OR THE 5TH HOUSE)

Saturn in Leo or the 5th—or ruling or co-ruling the 5th; or hard aspects from Saturn to any planets in the 5th.

This placement indicates a father who may be strict, or an older father. Children may be few, there may be no children, or children may require a good deal of sacrifice—this may be one's own children or other people's, as in the case of a teacher. Life may sometimes lack enjoyment, and spontaneity may be curtailed. If pleasure is suppressed for any reason, life becomes heavy and it is impossible for these people to express or feel enjoyment or happiness in anything they do. Jealousy and repressed anger are directed at others, who seem to restrict and stop these people from receiving the happiness they desire. For this reason they need to accept the limitations that appear to come from others and to harness their strength of will—which is considerable—in search of their deeper hidden self.

Once they learn to love and appreciate themselves and once they stop looking for approval, applause, or approbation from outside, much growth can occur. Aspects to the Sun need to be understood in respect to this. The positive expression of Saturn in this house is a fine sense of honor and self-assurance. This often comes later in life as these people eventually come to recognize that all strength, all happiness, all joy, and all completeness can never come from anything or anyone until they find and accept it within themselves. (See Saturn and Love, page 43.)

SATURN IN VIRGO (OR THE 6TH HOUSE)

Saturn in Virgo or the 6th house—or ruling or co-ruling the 6th; or hard aspects from Saturn to any planet in the 6th.

These people often feel less than perfect in the eyes of others. There may be a methodical mind, prudence, and practical ability. However, at times this may turn in on itself, causing a fault-finding tendency directed at one's own efforts or efforts connected to co-workers or those in one's employ. This fault-finding tendency can bring a nagging analysis to work and service of all kinds. There is often much anxiety, which, when severely aspected, causes illnesses both physical and mental. In some cases this position will cause people to become workaholics, where they will often be tied to service that requires most of their time and effort. In other cases, this will produce work-shy persons who are completely unable to harness their energies in connection with any employ. Both instances are negative expressions of Saturn.

Service of all kinds can become slavery, but only if these people refuse to use their analytical powers to examine their true inner nature. Now for some reason this is very difficult to do, as criticism from within or without causes great dis-ease. So they take the line of least resistance, and either keep their noses to the grindstone or create real reasons why they should not work. If true values connected to work and service can be found to dedicate their lives to—service which is a true reflection of their inner needs—then these individuals have much to offer the world. Criticism should be viewed in a positive light—fears and despondencies recognized and understood. As they move more and more to an alignment of mind, body, and emotions, this is reflected back in service and help to others, which, in turn, brings much inner peace and stabilization.

SATURN IN LIBRA (OR THE 7TH HOUSE)

Saturn in Libra or the 7th—or ruling or co-ruling the 7th; or hard aspects from Saturn to any planets in the 7th.

There is a feeling that wholeness can only be achieved through union with another, and close relationships become important as this person will look for strength through others. The message in this position of Saturn is that until the person assumes personal strength, he or she will continually feel let down by other people, particularly the spouse, as others people may become a burden or cause hardship in some way. Occasionally there is a late marriage, a large age difference between marriage partners, or this person feels comfortable and safe with responsible or older people. Sometimes a desire for partnerships may be suppressed, causing depression and loneliness. There is nearly always a shyness and reserve when in the company of someone of short acquaintance.

The positive side of Saturn's placement here is shown in tolerance, kindness, patience, reason, and good judgment in relating to others—particularly the partner. Saturn is exalted in Libra and offers an opportunity for an integration and balancing of opposites within the psyche—a uniting of the male and female principles, a blending of spirit and matter in its highest form. Those with this placement often go through very disappointing and painful episodes in connection to relationships, both personal and otherwise, before realizing that all they see within others is but a reflection of their own psyche. When they learn to let go of expectations and dependencies—plus any insincerity or intolerance within themselves—and learn the real meaning of responsibility in regard to everyone they meet, then all they seek within others will become part of themselves.

SATURN IN SCORPIO (OR THE 8TH HOUSE)

Saturn in Scorpio or the 8th house—or ruling or co-ruling the 8th; or hard aspects from Saturn to any planets in the 8th.

"Thoughts that do often lie too deep for tears",[7] can be found with this placement of Saturn, and such is the depth of feeling that this person often

---

[7] William Wordsworth, "Intimations of Immortality," verse XI, line 17.

prefers to hide a large part of himself. Hence there is usually a strong reserve with a tendency to brooding and secretiveness. The emotions are very deep but suppressed, and sexual inhibitions can cause differing modes of behavior. There may be difficulty connected to physical sexual expression, particularly in a female's chart; other areas of the chart should be looked at for a fuller explanation. In a male's chart there may also be a lack of sexual expression due to inhibitions. Some people may have a very active sex life, almost as if trying to compensate for their fear by this behavior. This is a very difficult placement of Saturn to investigate, particularly for a man, as there can be much suppression of feeling, which is often buried so deep and has such painful emotions attached that people may prefer not to look. A lack of flexibility is also common, but business sense is often sharp and executive ability may be in evidence—particularly in the financial affairs of others—although there may be stressful experiences concerned with divorce settlements, inheritance, other people's money, or similar matters.

Investigation into all areas concerned with transformation, as found in depth psychology, research into death and rebirth, plus recognizing the importance of other people's values, can do much to further these people's growth. To look at emotional and sexual needs realistically can bestow many blessings and illuminate many areas of misunderstanding and pain. Inquiring into psychology or astrology or other occult or hidden pathways may bring in the light and love so badly needed. To be reborn we undoubtedly need to go through the pain of death first, but this need not be in the terrible way we fear, but through a thorough understanding and transformation of our own human nature.

SATURN IN SAGITTARIUS (OR THE 9TH HOUSE)

Saturn in Sagittarius or the 9th—or ruling or co-ruling the 9th; or hard aspects from Saturn to any planet in the 9th.

In this placement of Saturn, there is often the need for additional education that for some reason does not materialize and this causes feelings of inferiority—as in the case of someone who could not go to college or university, or begins some study that has to be terminated before its completion. Frequently the need to expand and the need to hang on to something secure conflict, and when the individual does feel ready to step boldly into life, he or she can frequently overdo the exercise. Somehow the need to expand must co-exist with the duty and moral obligation laid down by Saturn. Natal aspects to Jupiter, particularly the harder ones, show where things may be overdone and where over-expansion may occur. Saturn in this position can become a god to fear, and guilt from early childhood memories may be generated. Hard aspects to Saturn will show where the area of apprehension and guilt may manifest.

These people greatly desire freedom but are unsure of how to obtain it and will often go to great lengths to liberate themselves from the imagined confines of others. They wish to understand true freedom and seek liberty often at great cost to themselves and those close to them. Serious thinking accompanies this position, especially on questions of philosophy, religion, and moral values and there may be a lifelong search for a true faith to base their lives on. At certain times, however, some kind of disillusion is attached to religious or philosophical questions. When these people understand that each and every answer to all philosophical, moral, and ethical questions must be found within themselves, they find the freedom they so earnestly desire.

SATURN IN CAPRICORN (OR THE 10TH HOUSE)

Saturn in Capricorn or the 10th—or ruling or co-ruling the 10th, conjunct or in hard aspect to the midheaven; or hard aspects from Saturn to any planets in the 10th.

There is often ambition demanding recognition with this placement, but the need to achieve can become over-important and sometimes destructive. In the case of a woman, part of this "shadow" can be projected on to the partner who then assumes the role. Responsibility can be carried to the extreme. This may be in pursuit of worldly ambition or, somehow or other, tied to "doing one's duty," in a negative and self-destructive way, and as a result of this self-inflicted duty, depression can occur. Pessimism is often prevalent as is hardness and a stern thriftiness in managing resources. The world, and all that's in it can at times seem hostile, and hence there can be a deep need to "beat" this society. There may be a fear of failure, and the need for recognition and respect within the social order, resulting in taking on more responsibility and obligations than can sometimes comfortably be handled. There can be a love of power, but this may only be to compensate for a sense of personal inadequacy in the eyes of the world.

When they stop trying to prove themselves and their capabilities, and cease to look at the world with a self-righteous attitude, where others are often condemned, these people start to gain ground. They learn to stop managing everyone around them, and focus on their real needs. To do this they must do a great deal of work on themselves and recognize the One they should give their service to. Saturn in this position can take on the guise of a wise teacher or an extremely hard jailer. Once the persevering spirit and sense of discipline are directed inward there is nothing in the realm of possibility that can truly stop them conquering their world where all their needs will be met—but until the will is directed to a spiritual purpose, they will remain forever disappointed.

SATURN IN AQUARIUS (OR THE 11TH HOUSE)

Saturn in Aquarius or in the 11th—or ruling or co-ruling the 11th; or hard aspects from Saturn to any planets in the 11th house.

There is usually a feeling of loneliness connected to this position, with long periods of time spent alone—this feeling also occurs when the person is lonely even among others. This is often an independent position, ideals are important and superficiality is not easily tolerated—although there may be periods in life when this is put up with to keep the peace. A certain shyness and often a shortage of real friends is common. People with this position of Saturn would like to feel they have friends they can count on, but often the opposite occurs and they are left feeling lonely and disillusioned. Some with this position compensate for feeling alone by participating in many social activities, with the aim of belonging to a group. Their lives are seemingly a whirl of activity, but this is only an outward show to keep away the fear of being alone with themselves, and in no way tackles the real problem—which comes from deep within. The danger here is that one group of friends with superficial values may be exchanged for a group appearing very different—but is just the same underneath.

When aspirations are truly and sincerely raised to a higher level, and responsibility is taken for oneself within the group experience, and the superficiality of modern living is looked at with a clear perspective, one starts to gain ground. Friends are discovered whose principles reach to a higher level of awareness than the commonplace. Groups and societies become more important as one starts to let go of more personal and emotional needs, for it is through association with others who share a common dedication to humanity that one comes to value personal identity. Sadly, the person who cannot find the more universal levels of friendship is destined to continue a lonely life. But the one who raises his or her eyes from the common ground of emotional need—and the need to belong to a social group—moves to a higher level of shared and universal friendship. When one lets go of the need to gratify the ego through superficial friendships and social orders, and instead directs this energy toward a collective cause, such as the search for a different set of social values and a greater understanding of society and its true purpose, then the person with this placement becomes well blessed with the gift of divine sharing and spiritual brotherhood.

SATURN IN PISCES (OR THE 12TH HOUSE)

Saturn in Pisces or the 12th—or ruling or co-ruling the 12th; or hard aspects from Saturn to any planets in the 12th.

This placement indicates fear and a lack of courage, with a tendency to depression at times. Intuition is usually very strong, but sensitivity and worry also occur. This person will often give in to existing conditions without trying to improve them in any way. Sorrows may often be hidden from others, and there is frequently a need for seclusion. Isolation, imprisonment, or self-imposed restriction is common—such as that found with long illnesses that cause loneliness and loss of contact with others, certain phobias, heavy business duties that take away almost all life and energy, a commitment to others such as people in the helping professions experience, a commitment that takes all one's time and strength, or the need to look after a sick relative. There may be other types of imprisonment such as those found by the unemployed who have no money and are locked within their four lonely walls.

This placement does seem to demand that sacrifices are made in some area, but whether this is the sacrifice of false martyrdom or true sacrifice made through universal compassion has to be determined. Giving must not be ego-based. If it is, these people will be continually disappointed, as they will never receive satisfaction or thanks from others that will bolster any ego-centered ideas or selfish aspirations. Punishment does seem to play a large part in the lives of these people, and others' acts of selfishness can cause much agony, but only because their own giving was ego-orientated. To learn to recognize their own spiritual need is important, and to set about improving their lives based on an understanding of universal principles. For this we must learn faith and understand that "all is one." We must stop seeing ourselves as separate, and, as we experience the pain of the world, we develop compassion and step closer to the infinite where self-imposed shackles are dissolved.

Working with the Saturn Meditation

Without doubt, Saturn brings necessary disciplines, limitations, and restrictions into our lives. However, in some instances the restriction can turn in on itself causing pain and isolation until the real truth of Saturn's message is comprehended. If we learn how to work with the Saturn energy within our own life, we can start to free ourselves from old habits and thought patterns that have limited our personal growth. Wherever Saturn occurs in a birth chart, there are limitations connected; these contain valuable lessons that are essential within our development.

> It is remarkable that Saturn causes effort to be aroused in all those who would use his vibration for the achievement of whatever goal the soul may be seeking. He increases the load of all who are pilgrims in any sense of the word, and he is thus said to represent a carrier of burdens, the greatest burden of all being responsibility; but in the very task that Saturn sets for each of his children there is the surety of each virtue he bestows bringing its own reward.[8]

SATURN AND PLANETARY ENERGY

In order to use the Saturn Meditation, an understanding is necessary of how planetary energies—and the Saturn energy in particular—work. The definition of a planetary energy can be explained in different ways depending on one's viewpoint. Jung calls them archetypal energies and sees them as forming the collective unconscious. Plato and the ancient Greeks called

---

[8] Alan Leo, *The Art of Synthesis*, p. 91.

them daemons as did Dante—they saw them as both a positive and negative force affecting human destiny. Plato said, however, that there was some choice in this: for although pain, fear, and other feelings are given to people by necessity, if they conquered the feelings they would live righteously, but if they were conquered by them, unrighteously. These energies emanating from the planetary intelligences are natural forces causing both positive and negative reactions.

Greek myths, recorded in classical Latin literature and attributed at that time to the Babylonians, linked certain gods with certain planets. It was said that the gods influenced human destiny through these planetary channels, and that human will was also connected and proportioned according to the planets' movement in the heavens. To the Romans, Saturn, known as the father of the Gods, was a god of plenty who ruled over a golden age where life was easy and gentle, although we know, of course, that there was much suffering under the Roman rule.

Theosophy teaches that before humans took on material bodies (brought into creation by Saturn as god of structure and form), we existed in a purely astral shape. This was before the fall into material life, as those who believed in Adam might say.[9]

As the story goes after the fall, Zeus (or Jupiter) continually made life hard for Saturn, who retaliated with a restraining hand. Saturn thus took on the significance of a restricting influence to mankind. This influence did not allow humanity to forget how much we needed to learn. Saturn, as the god who teaches us, inevitably, also has the image of a hard taskmaster who causes restriction, gloom, despair, and despondency as he works.

If we work with the Saturn energy and recognize how it influences our lives, we can develop an inner dialogue with this god; and we can learn to use Saturn's positive aspect. It will not remove responsibilities, but it will indicate areas connected to restriction and inferiority, which need to be accepted and understood.

No person, circumstance, or thing can take away our personal responsibility. No amount of money can compensate for our own inadequacy. You only have to look at some of the people who have money, yet

---

[9] Madame Blavatsky in *The Secret Doctrine*, discussed the fall: "It is universal tradition that, before the physiological "Fall," propagation of one's kind, whether human or animal, took place through the WILL of the creators, or of their progeny. It was the Fall of spirit into generation, not the Fall of mortal man" (Book 1, p. 192).

who have such difficulty coping with life, to support this. It seems that by thinking that things outside ourselves can compensate us for our own inadequacies, we cause those same inadequacies to grow larger.

Material success, or recognition of our success by others, does not necessarily mean we have got things right. The ability to be in charge of others does not always mean we are aware of our own inner motivations or that we are using our intellectual capacity and understanding with the moral integrity we should. It is often not until life becomes so uncomfortable with breakdowns, neurosis, or illness, that we realize there may be something wrong with that lifestyle, and, even then, many people will still refuse to accept their own part in what has happened.

In *The Inner World of Choice* Frances Wickes distinguishes the dilemma:

> God says, "Choose what you will and pay for it." We choose; we try to bargain with this mysterious god, secretly expecting him to give back our money if we do not like what we have chosen. But in merciless wisdom, he…exacts full payment, through which new consciousness may be born and a step toward wholeness taken. Hardened by defeat, confronted by his own weakness, tempered by the very injustice of life, man is thrown back upon himself and begins to see the nature of and the reasons for his choices. The payments then become the means of his learning how to choose.[10]

Always remember Saturn supplies the structure and framework that the Soul seeks—for without structure, no building can commence. In order to do this, he takes on the role of the planetary teacher, who bestows on us the apparent hardships, restrictions, and inadequacies that are necessary lessons for us. But at the same time—if we can only believe it— he gives us the choice of becoming positive creators. Working with Saturn can show us that all we experience comes from within, and is only there to teach us something important we need to learn. Apparent unkindnesses from others, inferiority complexes, others' domination, difficulties in the world, at work, or at home, and many other painful experiences only affect us because of our need to see and acknowledge where lawful structure is

---

[10] Frances Wickes, *The Inner World of Choice* (Boston: Sigo Press, 1988), p. 2. Printed with permission of Sigo Press, from: Inner World of Choice, by Francis Wickes, Copyright December, 1988.

necessary within our lives. We may also start to recognize the fact that people with wisdom do not always take the easy way out, and that they give back to the world as much as they take from it.

When the Saturn energy is used in a guided imagery form, it is possible to tap into an area that can both guide and teach us to use our own power and will, and to realize the truth of our own existence in the most natural and trustworthy way. Saturn should be seen as a planet of wisdom rather than limitation—as a teacher rather than a jailer. Liz Greene sums it up:

> A symbol of the psychic process, natural to all human beings, by which an individual may utilize the experiences of pain, restriction, and discipline as a means for greater consciousness and fulfillment...it is through him alone that we may achieve eventual freedom and self-understanding. [11]

The following examples are from one of the earliest Saturn workshops I did. Most of the people there had no knowledge of astrology and had done very little, if any, inner work before. Some of the astrological information given does not have a birth time. None of the group had done the Saturn Meditation before. (See Saturn Meditation on pages 77-85.)

• • •

Jean had Saturn conjunct Jupiter in Taurus squaring Mercury conjunct Mars in Leo. She asked Saturn: "Why do I have such a desperate inadequacy trying to express myself?"

In the hall it was pleasant, but the people made her feel very inferior. Saturn was saintly, kind and relaxed. Jean felt like a frail, small child. Her gift was a basket of fresh fruit—he was not impressed. Saturn gave her a book of wisdom. As Saturn she saw the people as ONE—and Jean as equal. Saturn wanted to help. He also gave her a pendant in the shape of a triangle which represented Mind, Body and Spirit.

• • •

Nichola wanted to find herself. She had Saturn conjunct the Moon in Aries. Saturn was also trine the Sun conjunct Pluto in Leo.

---

[11] Liz Greene, *Saturn: A New Look at an Old Devil* (London: Arkana, 1976 and York Beach, ME: Samuel Weiser, 1990), p. 10.

In the hall something was very threatening—she felt very afraid. Saturn was Christ-like—she was not afraid of him. She gave him a book. He was kind, loving and peaceful. As Saturn, Nichola felt strong, kind and gentle. She saw herself as being impatient—wanting to get ahead, but feeling others were restricting her—all there were on the same path, searching for truth. Saturn wants to help—he gives peace and love in the form of an orb and scepter. He says, "Come back anytime."

• • •

Olivia had a terrible inferiority complex. She asked, "Help me to be Me."

Her Saturn was in Capricorn in the 7th square the Sun in the 5th and the Moon in the 11th and opposing Mars and the Ascendant. The hall was medieval—the people were laughing, joking and enjoying themselves—she felt left out and lonely and very small. Saturn was big, refined-looking with a beard. She did not know if she liked him. Said he seemed unapproachable. She asked if he would be her friend. He said, "We are all friends." Olivia now starts to feel very panicky. She becomes Saturn. She sees herself as small—timid, frightened, looking very pitiful. As Saturn, she feels strong and in command—confident and happy—very relaxed. Becoming Olivia again, she keeps the feeling of strength—feeling taller, important, relaxed, happy and proud. Everyone in Saturn's hall is so happy—and so is Olivia.

• • •

Sara asks, "Why have I had to suffer like this?" She has a grand cross; Saturn in Scorpio in the 12th opposing the Sun and Mercury in Taurus in the 6th, and square Mars in Aquarius in the 3rd and Jupiter in Leo in the 10th, also a semi-square to the Moon in Libra in the 11th.

She saw Saturn as large—although not afraid, she was awe-inspired. She said, "I feel he is very just, although his means of ruling are harsh."

Saturn says to Sara, "Yours is not an easy path—but you will find the way if you have courage—I rule over the pathway that is not easy." She sees him as being wise and strong. As Saturn, Sara feels very powerful—feeling she understands. Becoming Sara again she asks him, "Have I learned, am I on the right path?" He replies, "Yes but you must wait for a little more time to pass." He gives her a bean representing new growth. He puts the bean in her subconscious. He says, "Work and be my friend—trust me more. My way appears harsh; but because you fight, you misunderstand." He winks, and continues, "You must not keep fighting me—you cannot avoid me. Do not forget what I say."

The general feeling of the group members about the Saturn experience was positive. Many realized things about themselves they had not been aware of before and experienced insights that were beyond their ordinary comprehension. Afterwards they all recorded a feeling of relief and any initial fear or negativity quickly receded. Working with Saturn can be both beneficial and fulfilling. It is a planet with a purpose for us all.

SATURN IN RELATIONSHIPS

Many concepts about intimate relationships have altered over the last few years, mainly due to a more permissive society. But there are still misconceptions and difficulties connected to romance and the quest for the "right partner," even with all the so-called understanding and self-awareness this era has brought. Why do we need close intimate relations with others, and what mechanism draws to us certain types of people?

Throughout history, men and women have searched for that elusive ideal mate, and probably few have succeeded in their search since they seek an ideal and perfect image, and other human beings are neither perfect nor ideal. They are simply human, with all the weaknesses that this implies. Every individual has a concept of perfection—needs to be met by the projected partner in question—and even those needs will change as the individual changes over the years.

Why do some people work so hard at relationships while others appear not to bother at all? It is true that all relationships go through testing periods, but surviving the test is an individual thing. You can never change another person—only yourself, which may be a radically different approach to the one most of us take: trying to persuade people to our own way of thinking. Unfairly it may seem that only one partner is trying, but the rewards for individual effort are greater than we can fully appreciate at first glance.

All the trials we experience in relationships are inevitable. For when we are challenged by others, we have to make choices, and these choices require an inner awareness and responsibility.

> Responsibility could easily deteriorate into domination and possessiveness were it not for the third component of love, *respect*. Respect is not fear and awe; it denotes, in accordance with the root of the word (*respicere*—to look at), the ability to see a person as he is, to be aware of his unique individuality. Respect means concern that the other person should grow and unfold as he is. Respect, thus, implies the absence of exploitation. I want the loved person to grow and unfold for his own sake, and in his own ways, and not for the purpose of serving me. If I love the other person, I feel one with him or her, but with him *as he is*, not as I need him to be as an object for my use. It is clear that respect is possible only if *I* have achieved independence; if I can stand and walk without needing crutches, without having to dominate and exploit anyone else. Respect exists only on the basis of freedom: "l'amour est l'enfant de la liberté" as an old French song says; love is the child of freedom, never that of domination.[12]

If you have any knowledge of astrology, you become aware that how you feel, what you experience, and what you draw to yourself from others, can be found to be the result of energies interacting on the placing of planets at birth. So, to benefit yourself and others it makes sense to learn to understand these energies. There is a lesson to be learned from the interactions of these energies whether you are a student of astrology or not.

In the planetary system, Saturn links our personal natures with those of the heavens, and by communicating with the Saturn energy, you can learn that which you need to "learn to do gladly…" (*Jung*). In other words, lower will can be linked to higher nature and by doing this, and working on and transforming yourself, you will begin to release negative thought

---

[12] Eric Fromm, *The Art of Loving* (New York: HarperCollins, 1956; London: Unwin, 1975), p. 28.

patterns you have developed to protect yourself, and discover areas that need further investigation within the psyche.

However, there should be no martyr complex in all this! Any feelings of superiority—in particular superiority to partners who have not become involved in such deep inner work—can only add fuel to the fires of self-deception. The sign of true growth is the acceptance of our partners as they are, not as we would like them to be.

It is recognized in Jungian psychology that the psyche contains a shadow—the part of ourselves both positive and negative we have decided is not us. Some say the shadow is half of the whole personality, a hidden part of us that we project onto a partner. In every woman there lives an inner man—the animus; and in every man, an inner woman—the anima. These constitute the male and female seeking to unite within the individual psyche.

You have possibly met people who seem friendly, generous, charming, and hospitable, yet they complain that their partner is unfriendly and difficult. If they change partners, a similar pattern occurs, or it could be that seemingly strong, confident individuals marry weak ones who they have to support in some way. There are many combinations but always the inner shadow, the anima or animus—the hidden partner—will seek a reflection of itself in the other! Each and every time, there is something deep within us that draws a partner that is similar to our partner within.

By seeking to grow and transform ourselves, we allow our hidden partner to grow and transform also. This cannot fail to change our relationship with the shadow's human counterpart, our mate, in a positive way. It is interesting to note that when a person has left a partner and has found a new mate, the ex-partner will usually take on all the negative shadow projection and the new partner will assume most of the positive.

But when this new relationship matures, the negative shadow begins to be projected on to the second partner and history is repeated. Unless certain things hidden within the psyche have been worked through, they will cause trouble in time. Until we accept responsibility for ourselves and our shadow side, the projections will go on.

The 7th house and Saturn are close companions when viewed in connection to the "other person." To find our shadow partner, we must look at the 7th house, the planets there, their aspects, the ruler of the 7th house, its position in the chart, and the aspects it receives from other planets. The Sun and Mars are important in a female chart when viewing the male partner, and the Moon and Venus in a male chart when viewing the female partner. These planetary energies within an intimate relationship bring both positive and negative influences and are interchanged between the people involved. Steinbrecher in his book *The Inner Guide Meditation* calls it "shadow dancing" as each partner dances to the unconscious projection of the other.[13]

Saturn will challenge the very structure on which a relationship is built. Through pain, suffering, loneliness, and guilt, he forces us to discover who we really are. The more we deny his demands and seek some romantic dream where we all have our own way and live happily ever after, the more he will plague us until we begin to realize what love really is and that we have to develop union on an inner level before we ever can understand it.

• • •

Take the case of Richard, 40 years old, an advertising executive and family man. Richard was based in Edinburgh, but his job took him all over the world. His wife, Anna, ran his home, raised his two children, and enjoyed a luxury lifestyle but had to accept her husband's frequent absences. To Richard, they seemed happy enough since she seemed content with the many material comforts he was able to give her. Richard reveled in his go-getting career and felt that he gave his wife and family everything they needed within the time he had at his disposal. In fact, he appreciated his domestic interludes the more because they gave him peace and security in the middle of a frantic lifestyle.

Richard had girlfriends but never a real affair. The women in his life were companions for an evening, but never important enough to be anything more. Anna always came first after his career. Therefore, he was devastated when he arrived home one evening to find her gone and a letter tucked by the telephone. Anna had packed her belongings and gone off with a local builder. The children were safely at boarding school; the house deserted. He was bewildered: she had given no warning, no ultimatum. Why would she do this to him?

---

[13] Edwin Steinbrecher, *The Inner Guide Meditation* (London: Aquarian Press, 1988 and York Beach, ME: Samuel Weiser, 1988), p. 137.

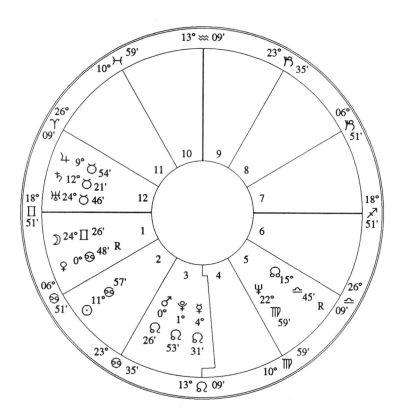

Chart 1. Richard. Birth data from family has been withheld for confidentiality. Chart calculated with Placidus Houses, using Nova/Printwheels.

When Richard sought counseling, it became quite apparent that Anna had become weary of coming second to his career. The comfortable lifestyle was just a veneer; beneath it, the actual structure of their marriage was very shaky. Richard decided to work on himself and booked some self-awareness courses, hoping that if he could change himself, he might win her back.

But time and his career got in the way again. Richard canceled the courses and instead opted to propose to his secretary! He had known Jan for three years and throughout this last difficult period she had been a good friend and a great source of comfort and strength. Jan, who seemed to worship her highly successful boss, was surprised and flattered and prompt-ly accepted. They were married within six months. After four weeks, Richard was desperately seeking counseling again.

The marriage was a disaster. Engineered on the rebound, it had not been thoroughly thought out by either partner. For Richard, it was simply a means of restoring the security of domestic life, but for Jan, it was a marriage to her dream—a tough, glamorous executive. What neither of them realized was that they were each projecting onto the other the positive illusion of the shadow. Neither of them actually wanted—or saw—what they got.

Marital history was repeating itself. Richard's first marriage had failed for the same reason. He had projected upon Anna certain aspects of his shadow that were nurturing, caring, and domestic. Richard's chart (see Chart 1) shows the Moon in Gemini conjunct Venus in Cancer, both in the 1st house, and both squaring Neptune in the 5th (Neptune co-ruled the 10th), which showed a false idea of his own and his partner's emotional needs and an erroneous belief in what a woman should be. His 7th house is empty: Sagittarius is on the cusp, its ruler Jupiter conjuncts Saturn in the 12th in Taurus, which sextiles the Sun in Cancer in the 2nd, but Jupiter squares a Mercury-Mars-Pluto conjunction in Leo in the 3rd. Saturn rules the 8th and 9th houses. Anna had not been fulfilled in the role that had been cast for her. It is difficult to ascertain exactly what she had projected onto Richard as her birth time is unknown, and she did not come for therapy. In her solar chart (see Chart 2 on page 42), her Sun in Aries squared Saturn in Cancer, which indicated both a lack of confidence and lack of emotional

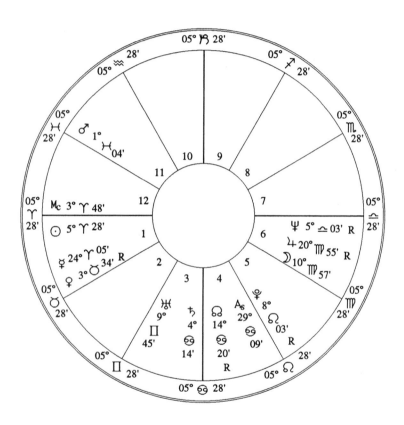

Chart 2. Anna. Birth data from family has been withheld for confidentiality. Chart calculated with Placidus Houses, using Nova/Printwheels.

fulfillment. The Sun also trined Uranus in Gemini, opposed Neptune in Libra, and trined Pluto in Leo. Mars in Pisces trined Saturn but squared Uranus.

Now, second-time around, Richard found himself in an even more difficult situation. Jan was projecting upon him her positive image of an exciting, powerful, and dominant personality. Her chart (Chart 3 on page 44) shows Uranus in Cancer exactly on the 7th house cusp, with Pluto in Leo also in the 7th. Its ruler the Moon is in Scorpio in the 10th and squares a Venus-Jupiter conjunction in Aquarius in the 1st. Her Sun is in Sagittarius in the 12th, squaring a Mars-Saturn conjunction in Virgo in the 8th. The Sun also trines Pluto, the Mars-Saturn conjunction squares Uranus, Saturn rules her 1st house. The power and excitement she saw in Richard was *her* power, not his, and he projected upon her a domestic role she could not play, and which she found impossible to fulfill emotionally.

Looking at the two charts it is easy to see how Richard's inner woman was projected on to Jan, and how her inner man was projected on to him. They were not prepared for all the difficulties within themselves that needed acknowledgment and acceptance, difficulties they did not like when they saw them reflected in the other. Both were disappointed with what they got and blamed the other, instead of looking to where the real difficulties lay.

If Richard had not canceled those courses and if he had sought to know himself better, he might not have made such a disastrous second match. Having made mistakes the first time around, it would have helped him if he had faced his own shadow partner, thereby seeing his problems in a clearer context and perhaps avoiding making the same mistakes again.

SATURN AND LOVE

When we look at our world history and particularly at the events of the twentieth century, it makes sense for us to try to understand love more— both in a personal as well as in a collective sense—or else we will continue to be ruled by hostility and suspicion.

What is love? Poets, artists, writers, and musicians through the ages have tried to define it, to delineate this mysterious state. William Blake's description of love expresses a very free and joyous experience.

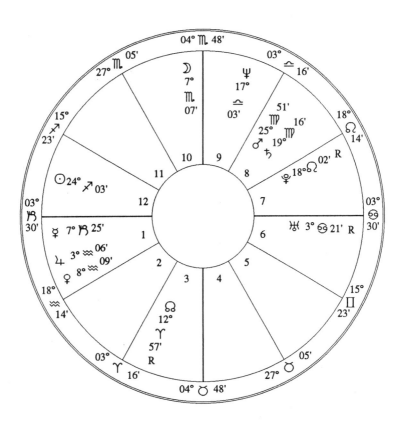

Chart 3. Jan. Birth data from family has been withheld for confidentiality. Chart calculated with Placidus Houses, using Nova/Printwheels.

Love to faults is always blind
Always is to joy inclined
Lawless winged and unconfined
And breaks all chains from every mind.[14]

Venus will show the urge for harmonious relations within the chart: how we relate to and attract others, our love of beauty and lovely things, that which attracts us. But the region of the chart that will show how we express the self and accept love and enjoyment from others is the 5th house. Saturn in Leo or the 5th house, or ruling the 5th, or making difficult aspects to any planets there can often cause difficulties in this area of experience.[15]

In astrology, Leo rules the heart, and it is the heart we are talking about. Do we achieve our heart's desire, do we express what is in our hearts, are our hearts at ease? We say: "He has no heart," or "My heart is broken." There is a joyous childlike quality connected to the 5th house, and Saturn will restrict it, causing the inner child to demand endless attention within the psyche (psyche meaning mind and/or emotions). We must remember love cannot be felt or expressed until we learn to recognize and accept the part that functions through the heart. If we do not understand this concept, Saturn will place limits of one sort or another on our affections—how we love, how we accept affection from others, how much enjoyment we receive from others and, perhaps, too, on our expectations of these qualities.

Disappointments in love affairs and the affections seem to occur the most frequently in connection with Saturn, Leo and the 5th house. In this case, Saturn's role as shadow is to limit, repress, undermine, depress, and frighten the part of us that responds to or feels love. This is then experienced in the conscious mind and blamed on something the partner or the other person has or has not done; for instance, "He or she has not loved, respected, or approved of me enough, or shown me enough affection."

• • •

---

[14] William Blake, [How to Know Love From Deceit], from *The Complete Poems of William Blake,* edited by Alicia Ostriker (London: Penguin, 1977), p. 54.

[15] These difficulties can occur not only when reading Saturn in Leo or the 5th house as we do in this chapter, but also apply to Saturn ruling or co-ruling the 5th, or in hard aspect to any planet there.

When Andrew sought therapy, he explained that he had never really felt loved; although his marriage had survived eighteen years, most of the time it had been a struggle. Andrew's chart shows a well-aspected Venus in Libra in the 7th, but he has Saturn conjunct Pluto in Leo in the 6th house and ruling the 8th. He explained that for the last ten years he had suffered a painful and difficult illness, and the doctors had eventually made the diagnosis that it was psychosomatic which was why he sought therapy. The illness had made the intimate side of the marriage very difficult and strained. He felt his wife had never shown him any understanding and was not as sympathetic or supportive as she could be. He thought she blamed him for being ill. Each had become bitter and disappointed in their expectations: the more she criticized him, the less loved Andrew felt and the less inclined he was to try to improve relations. He also let his illness become an excuse for continually demanding attention, and when this was not forthcoming, Andrew blamed his wife for his condition. He refused to accept any responsibility for what was happening to him and stopped therapy after a few sessions.

Liz Greene describes how the process of restriction from Saturn works in Leo and the 5th house.

> The person with Saturn in the 5th house often demands so much from others that he is left lonely and heartbroken. He is capable of much love and devotion but dare not express it without asking for a guarantee back: only when he recognizes this unconscious process of barter can he begin to free himself from it.[16]

Saturn in the 5th gives a decided lack of a sense of self so this person will, in some way, seek this from others. Yet ironically, others' love and approval will never fill the void within. There is also the feeling of not being appreciated for one's self, and an emptiness inside that is never filled by the other person.

• • •

David was a professional writer and artist in his mid-30s with high academic qualifications, a strong sense of humor, sociable manners, and not

---

[16] Liz Greene, *Saturn: A New Look at an Old Devil*, p. 84.

a little ambition. He enjoyed a successful lifestyle with his own home, a circle of friends, and interests that included theater, music, and traveling. So why did he need help? David was successful, but behind the easygoing charm he was suffering. He felt like a failure: a series of relationships had all turned sour on him. He was not a superficial man and always sought girlfriends who could be potential partners rather than casual affairs. In most cases he had been left hurt and bewildered by partners whom he said always seemed to criticize him: he was too dull, too fat, too old-fashioned. Women also apparently rejected him for other men who seemed to be what he was not, and David had hidden the pain of rejection behind a brave facade. In the last instance, he had become involved with a woman of a different faith. Once again, David felt inadequate and confused. She seemed to love him for himself, but he still felt he was not quite good enough.

During therapy David saw himself as a small and unwanted child, hurt and bewildered. That was the burden he was carrying subconsciously into every relationship; that was his expectation. David has Saturn in Virgo in the 5th (Chart 4, page 48), indicating a sensitivity to criticism, and lack of appreciation of self. Saturn ruling the 9th shows the possibility of religious difficulties, and ruling the 10th house also implies the need to achieve status in the world. The aspects to Saturn are a wide conjunction with Mars in the 5th, suggesting a need to put energy into affairs of the heart and a liking for entertainment and creative activity, but because of the conjunction with Saturn, the Mars energy was often blocked and frustrated. There is a wide opposition between Saturn and Jupiter in Pisces in the 11th house, which could imply that it is hard for David to achieve balance between friendships and love affairs.

It was suggested that David's small child should be taken to Saturn, to ask the following question. "What can my little boy do for you?" In David's words, this is what happened.

> The journey was easy, and when the gatekeeper opened the door, he was young and smiling, very relaxed, and friendly. I like him. Inside, the crowd are chanting something; they seem to be attentively standing in ranks. I see a woman I recognize and ask her what they are doing there.
>
> "Don't be silly," she says. "You know."

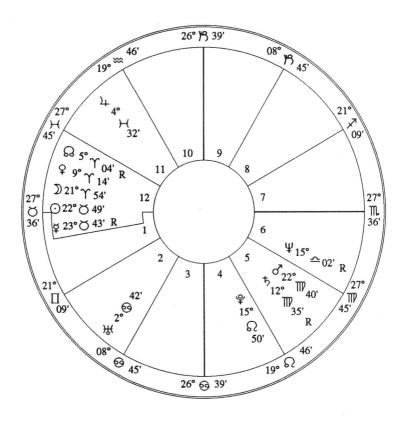

Chart 4. David. Birth data from family has been withheld for confidentiality. Chart calculated with Placidus Houses, using Nova/Printwheels.

"No I don't," I reply.

"Well, it's the place to be...it's all happening here, we're on our way up."

I tell her I think she has got it wrong. She insists that she hasn't as she has studied many years to be here. I ask someone else: "Excuse me, would you be kind enough to tell me why you're here?"

"It's the place to be," he says.

"For what, who are all these people?" I persist.

He looks puzzled and irritated. A voice somewhere says, "What you see are ghosts, memories, thoughts, desires, which are concentrated into people of your mind, parts of you, thought forms, attitudes, personalities; your life as lived."

This information makes me feel, not uneasy, but weary, and raises questions as to my responsibility regarding these images. I walk down the hall and pass through the crowd into an open space, which as I cross makes me very aware of my aloneness and produces a feeling of anxiety and fear. There are clouds of mist between Saturn and me (the crowd now seems a long way away). I come to the clouds and pass through. It is lighter here. Saturn is very large. I mean larger than I have ever seen him, and I'm thinking, "Why does he vary in size?"

"I am as you see me; as you need to see me," he says.

"Do I need to see you this big?" I ask skeptically.

"Indubitably," he replies. "How big should a god be?" He sits relaxed, calm, and concerned, with his hands folded in his lap. He makes me feel very welcome.

I give him my gift which is an uncut crystal that represents the barrier between myself and my child. I ask my question. "What can my little boy do for you?"

He replies, "Ah well, he can be you, for indeed, he is you, the best part of you. For him, you have come here; for him, I will take care of you. Waste not time, let him grow, protect him, nurture him, serve him, give him your place. Above all, learn to protect him, show him not to everyone, show him in your work, and not always in your dealings with others. Let them earn his respect and he will respond as is right. He can be himself for me; he is nearer you than all the others."

I start to think of the past.

He says, "Let the dead bury the dead. It is gone, it is no longer the present. Have faith and courage to allow the dead to be dead. Their path departs, continue, go on, live and trust in the moment completely. All is there."

I step into and become the god; I see David as someone who is beginning to mature becoming stronger and more together. I see the others as dead, wedded hopelessly to illusion. I give David an amulet, a talisman of protection and strength, to give him more confidence.

I step out of the god and become David again. As I look up at Saturn, he looks thoughtful. I feel confidence and courage. I thank him for his help, and take my leave. The gatekeeper is respectful in his attitude as he opens the door to let me out. I say to him that I will be back soon. He nods, smiles and shuts the door behind me.

Over the next few months, as David worked with the meditation, he grew visibly stronger and more sure of himself on a deep inner level, instead of seeking himself through others and through his achievements. He began to realize that the source of his strength was within. But not all people have this knowledge that David has gained. Liz Greene says,

> The person with Saturn in the 5th is sometimes not easy to love because he is like a jug with no bottom and absorbs affection and attention endlessly without being satisfied; however, if he begins to understand that his path is inward towards the self, he may begin to see what kind of opportunity is offered to him.[17]

---

[17] Liz Greene, *Saturn: A New Look at an Old Devil*, p. 85.

This love, approval, and sense of self must first be accepted on an inner level, because even if a person does find a really loving partner they will, at times, find it very difficult to believe in the love offered. And any crisis that occurs within the relationship will trigger off their sense of not being truly loved and will deepen their inadequacy still further.

• • •

Cathy's story was very sad. She had spent her life thinking she was a mistake. She was the youngest of eight children, and when her mother became ill, shortly after Cathy's birth, she had been sent to live with an aunt who lived far away. Her aunt's family ran a small farm, and at an early age, Cathy was expected to work. As she grew up she said she felt no more than an unpaid laborer. When she eventually married a steady, kindly man, she could not believe he loved her or held her in any esteem. She tortured herself constantly with the dread that he would leave her for someone else. She could never believe in his love. Cathy's husband brought her for therapy, because as he said, "Cathy is threatening to leave me, because she says I do not love her. Please help. I love her so much but she will not believe me." Cathy's chart (see Chart 5 on page 52) shows Saturn in Leo in the 6th in close conjunction with Mars and Pluto, which trines the Sun in Aries in the 1st, and sextiles Uranus in the 3rd. After a few sessions working with Saturn, Cathy began to develop confidence and to realize that the lack of love was indeed within her. She is now trying to understand herself on a much deeper level.

Similarly there are people who go from one love affair to another, always searching for that ideal lover. Each time they think they find him or her, but end up disillusioned, disappointed, and dissatisfied.

Jonathan ran a marketing firm which employed 500 women, and he was already in his fourth marriage by the time he sought counseling. He confessed that his life seemed to have followed a repeated pattern: each marriage had been to a much younger woman who apparently adored him, and then failed as the young woman matured into an individual with a mind of her own and a more critical attitude toward him. Then he felt threatened and unloved and always turned to a new girlfriend for solace and approval. At 45, the strain was beginning to show as he explained that his latest girlfriend was younger than his daughter. In his chart, Saturn was in Virgo

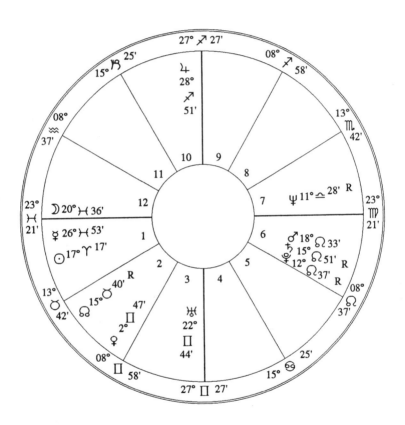

Chart 5. Cathy. Birth data from family has been withheld for confidentiality. Chart calculated with Placidus Houses, using Nova/Printwheels.

in the 5th, making no aspects to other planets, and ruling the 10th house, where Jupiter was positioned.

Daphne was in a very similar position. She was an artistic, creative lady in her 50s whose sculpting career was interspaced with short, sharp affairs. She wanted a relationship that was more stable and conventional but never seemed to achieve it. Daphne's chart has Saturn in the 7th, near the 8th house cusp, ruling the 5th. It squares Mercury in Sagittarius in the 4th and sextiles Jupiter in Capricorn in the 5th. She complained that when she got to know the men in her life, she found them weak.

It is interesting to note that artists' charts do sometimes show Saturn in or ruling the 5th. The 5th house is the house of creative expression, as well as love affairs; so you would think this placement would be detrimental to the artist's profession. Dane Rudhyar describes the test of the 5th house.

> In the 5th house the great test involves the ability to act out one's innermost nature in terms of purity of motive and using in a 'pure' manner the means available for the release of one's energies.[18]

If artists are truly inspired, they will surely give themselves to their creations—not for applause or recognition but for the sheer joy of creating. It is only when artists work for their art alone that Saturn gives his blessing; and so it must be.

When people with Saturn in the 5th stop looking for love, admiration, and guarantees outside of themselves, they will reach out to a higher principle, and learn to give and receive love from the very center of their beings. Then they will have recognized their "True Self." Whatever we want, we must want for the right reasons, and this must include love.

What is the True Self, and what has it to do with love? The True Self is the consciousness of the spirit—a child in the sense of innocence and naturalness, an inner wisdom that allows us to channel the energies of the spirit to create and inspire and allows a love that is secure in itself. This is a love free from the fears and entrapments of emotional and physical desire. This is not to say that we have to do without close emotional and physical involvements, but that these factors do not control the situation. The love

---

[18] Dane Rudhyar, *The Astrological Houses* (Sebastopol, CA: CRCS Publications, 1986), p. 84.

itself is supreme: it is the lord of the commitment made to a partner, child, lover, or any other person or ideal. Emotional and physical desires are only illusory, but love itself is beyond illusion, and thus must be true to itself. In this world of dreams, the only truth is love, and love is the only truth.

> *Love, is the only answer to an existence in plenitude.*
> *Is an inner state of profound sensitivity towards life.*
> *Is a joyful occasion that is celebrated when our mind rejects*
> *All deceitful prejudices and lies.*
> *That is why love is never immoral.*[19]

FINDING THE BALANCE WITH SATURN ENERGY

We have spoken of the 7th house as the house of the "other person," the partner and shadow. In older astrology this was also known as the house of open enemies. The 7th house is the natural house of Libra; the symbol of Libra is the scales which denote balance—so it becomes natural to seek balance from the Saturn phenomenon in connection to ourselves and others.

> It is the sign in which Saturn is said to be exalted or to have its greater power from the human standpoint. It denotes a well-balanced Will or Desire Nature, and coincides with the influence of Saturn as the Bridge between the higher and lower half of the heavens, taken as the ascent or descent from the one to the other. It also coincides with the idea of Saturn as the planet of Justice, holding the sword in one hand and the scales in the other. It is a decidedly critical influence, since it places the Will or Desire Nature in the balance between right and wrong, truth and falsehood.[20]

This is not just the balance of the Saturn energy, but the *ability to balance* all energies within the chart (although when working with Pluto, an additional

---

[19] Julio Roberto is a Portuguese poet. The author took this quote from a poster by Roberto.

[20] Alan Leo, *Saturn* (York Beach, ME: Samuel Weiser, 1970), p. 61.

exercise is useful; c.f. chapters on Pluto). Neptune in hard aspect will bring the potential for confusion and doubt in some area, especially when triggered off by transit or progression. This was the case with Robert.

When Robert came for therapy he appeared to be a very mind-orientated person, on the surface, who, until his illness, had been a successful professional man. Underlying this success was a deep sensitivity and an active psychic life that caused disturbing visions over which he appeared to have little control and that had caused the initial breakdown. He came for therapy after the breakdown, explaining how he needed help to throw light on his present situation—also more insight into the influences that caused it.

He was an attractive, friendly, likeable, and idealistic person, but deep down, he had little confidence and was continually disappointed in life and other people. However hard he tried, personal and professional relationships always proved very difficult and destructive and caused him much guilt and depression. In his lifelong search for a meaningful life philosophy, he always ended up confused, discouraged, and disillusioned. His Neptune in Virgo was exactly conjuncting the Ascendent and shows an analytical mind prone to unclear thinking in some areas and a confused self-image. See Chart 6, page 56.

Neptune was ruler of his Sun and Mercury which were in Pisces in the 8th. This could indicate an active imagination and interest in the occult. The 7th house Pisces Moon indicates a caring nature and need for emotional support from others, which probably did not materialize exactly as he required; for the Moon rules his 11th house, which contains a Mars-Pluto-Jupiter conjunction opposing Saturn in the 5th in Capricorn. Saturn is sextile the Moon, also the Sun and Mercury in the 8th, giving a direct and disciplined approach to any in-depth psychological thought. After several weeks of therapy, Robert took the following problems to Saturn:

1) Guilt—what is its purpose and what use is it?

2) Uncertainty, inadequacy, anxiety, and fear—why so much and how to deal with it?

3) I am trying to accept my limitations—so far a negative acceptance—how can I make this positive?

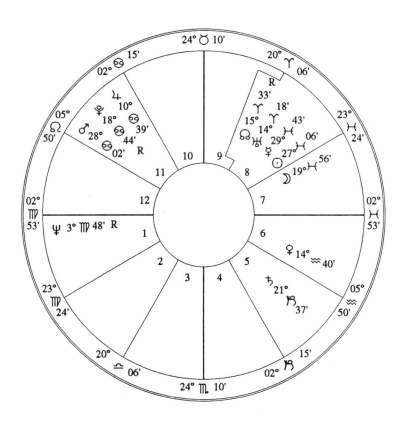

Chart 6. Robert. Birth data from family has been withheld for confidentiality. Chart calculated with Placidus Houses, using Nova/Printwheels.

His gift to Saturn was a bag of negatives—guilt, uncertainty, anxiety, and fear. He had the following experiences in his Saturn meditation.

> The gatekeeper is very swarthy in appearance with a sallow skin, clean-shaven, rather plump and short. He has a cheerful, open expression. He is dressed in an odd assortment of European and mid-eastern costume—Turkish trousers and blouse—European waistcoat and coat, no hat. He is middle aged. I don't dislike him though he's not the sort of person I would usually be easy with. He invites me in with an expansive gesture.
>
> Inside, there is a body of nuns. There is silence. They kneel down. There are also men there—some are priests, some monks, also mullahs and dervishes. Most stand in silence with hands crossed, some kneel. There is an air of serious attentive silence. I walk towards Saturn. The light is palest pearl grey and there is a scent I do not recognize. The floor is off-white marble: veined but with no mosaic pattern. I feel quite heavy. He looks very large, but as I approach, he gets smaller until when I arrive he is about eight feet tall.
>
> Saturn has Roman sandals with fur liners inside. In fact, he is dressed as a Roman centurian. He wears a white tunic beneath his breast plate, which is pewter colored. He is wearing a black cloak held at the shoulders. He is clean-shaven with a short Roman haircut—a bit like Augustus. His hair is white, his head bare. There is a severity in his appearance though not in his expression. He sits resting, holding the throne's arms in a relaxed way.
>
> I greet him—he graciously acknowledges—and I hand him a black plastic bag full of guilt, uncertainty, anxiety, and fear. He reaches slowly and majestically forward, grasps the bag, holding it up for inspection, nodding his approval, placing it in his lap and leaning slightly forward, links his hands. He waits to hear the question.
>
> "Guilt—what is its purpose and what use is it?"

Saturn replies, "Know that it (guilt) is the means by which men are paralyzed, shackled, kept in their imagined place of servitude by the devil who would control you all."

"And without guilt?" I ask.

"Man is free to serve who he will."

I ask, "But serve he must?"

"Not necessarily, not if his gifts demand that he does not. A distinction should be made between servitude-slavery and service-freedom. It is a question of finding your own balance. Man is free to serve in his own way. If he will not have this – which after all is Karmic—then, servitude. Find your way, be yourself. Things are so fashioned that this service *is* perfect freedom. Guilt is for those who will not find their own true path—and willingly tread it. Have no fear your time will come."

I ask, "Uncertainty, inadequacy, anxiety and fear, why so much and how to deal with it?"

"*So* much! It does not seem to me so much," Saturn replies. "Enough. Enough for you to understand it, know it, escape it and leave it. Free it; feel it; go toward it, explore it—and when it has given up its message it will dissolve."

"And in the past this has brought me to disaster—it certainly seemed too much," I tell him.

Saturn says, "Know this: that nothing is too much. It is what is karmically required at that time. It is, after all, the result of *what has gone before.*"

I ask, "I am trying to accept my present limitations: so far a negative acceptance. How can I make this positive? There is a message in there. How can I open to them/it?"

Saturn replies, "Now you are talking sense. Learn to *live:* To live out those restrictions. Explore them, know, experience their living quality." (At this point I begin to object.)

"I know, I know," Saturn continues. "Let it come, let it come to you. As it will if you refuse to escape: then it must open up. If you make no demand of the situation, if you make no conditions, if you accept and live it out, without escape, its message will be yours. *That* is freedom. That is the end of your limitations and the beginning of balance.

This makes me feel very hopeful. I become Saturn. I feel a great warmth and compassion and desire to help Robert. I am also patient—knowing time. I will support and help him all I can in his journey. I see someone grown patient, determined, mindful—a man—a very ordinary man. I see the others in the hall in exactly the same light—there is no pretending to *feel* or *be* what one is not. Now at last something is possible. I consider the gift that I give him. Strength is my gift. It is in the form of a Golden Eagle. I give it to him and tell him, "It is to rest on your shoulders."

I become Robert again. I am aware and feel his compassion.

He raises his hand in blessing and says, "Come again soon."

The gathered people seem very aware of me in an approving way. The gatekeeper is the same—very affable.

Robert begins to work with his Neptune placement and the rest of his chart, accepting that his active unconscious was a source of great creativity and growth, and that psychic activity need not be a source of conflict and fear if properly understood. He returned to a life where he could work with his innate creative ability, at his own pace and in his own time. Relationships also became a source of growth, once he realized his true potential. (He also worked with Pluto. See Part III, Pluto and Liberation of the Self, p. 148.)

• • •

We can also use the Meditation for difficulties connected to other planetary placements. By working with, and seeing through, the eyes of Saturn, we can use the energy for positive change and growth rather than destructive chaos.

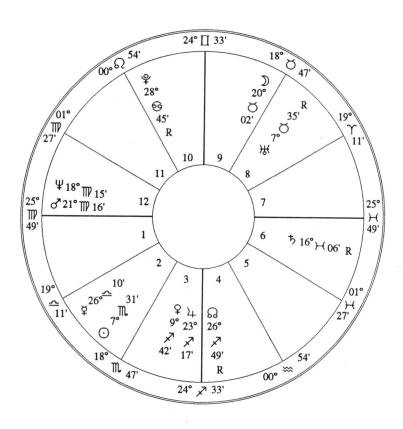

Chart 7. Anne. Birth data from family has been withheld for confidentiality. Chart calculated with Placidus Houses, using Nova/Printwheels.

Ann had spent her life escaping. Two marriages failed even though emotional involvement is important to her, and her present relationship was undergoing a serious crisis when she came for therapy. She worked from home, running a small restaurant, and had been experiencing difficulties with her children, as well as finding people in general very difficult to cope with. And although admitting to be deeply fond of her live-in partner—who was very supportive—she expressed a feeling of being hopelessly trapped. Now in her late 40s, she desperately wanted things to work out, but could not seem to find the balance in connection to herself, her emotional life, and her work. All she could think about was running away.

Her chart shows a Scorpio Sun in the 2nd house, opposing Uranus in Taurus in the 8th (see Chart 7), suggesting a need for freedom and change conflicting with inner values, security, and personal needs. She has a Mars-Neptune conjunction in Virgo in the 12th conjuncting the Ascendant showing that action taken was often unrealistic and not well thought out. This Mars-Neptune conjunction squares Jupiter in Sagittarius on the 4th house cusp, and also opposes Saturn in Pisces in the 6th, and is sesquiquadrate to Uranus in the 8th. It was when Uranus (by transit) triggered off this T-square, that Ann almost lost control. This was further aggravated by transiting Pluto moving in to conjunct the Sun and oppose Uranus. After explaining Ann's chart to her, she decided to use the Saturn Meditation.

Her first visit to Saturn was difficult, although the actual journey was easy. The gatekeeper was a Roman soldier. Ann tells him she is there to ask for help, and although he lets her in, she said, "He felt hostile."

The people in the hall had no faces, and it was very lonely there. Saturn looked very wise and seemed to be summing her up. She didn't like this and wanted to run; but she stayed and asked Saturn, "Will you help me and be my friend?"

He said, "I will, although it's rather late to ask."

Ann gives him a large stone, which symbolized her mind.

The second visit a week later was much more positive. Ann tells the gatekeeper she is here for "greater learning and understanding." He seems much friendlier as he lets her in. The hall was full of beautiful fair-haired people. Saturn welcomes Ann. She gives him more stones. He appreciates these and says, "I will be your friend as I see you are sincere."

She asks him, "How do I overcome anxiousness that comes with responsibility?"

He replies to this, "Try to relax and think of other things. There's no easy way: you would not be given responsibility unless you were capable of dealing with it. You will never escape. If you run it gets worse. Stay where you are and work it through."

Ann feels humble and understands what he means.

He continues, "Everything you want will come, you must be more patient, and learn to include other people in your life." All the people in the hall are listening and nodding. They like Ann.

She then walks into and becomes Saturn, and sees herself as a small person who will not look up—someone who is still trying to escape but is beginning to look like she wants to join the other people there. She steps down from the god and becomes Ann again, feeling Saturn is supporting her and taking away her tension and loneliness.

Saturn tells her, "Go forth and always stand upright, everything will follow. I give you *confidence* to be you. Now smile and be more gentle. I have put you on the path: follow it."

The people in the hall are pleased at this and start clapping. Ann takes her leave but feels very sad at going. She likes Saturn and all the people there.

Over the next few months, using the meditation, Ann works through her overwhelming need to escape. She emerges stronger in her relationship with her partner and better able to relate to other people in general.

• • •

Other difficulties either natally or by transit, can be defined the same way. Even Jupiter can manifest in negative ways: such as laziness and trying to take the easy way out—over-relating, over-spending, over-optimism or excessive reactions to any situation. Again, Saturn can show you how to balance these feelings if you choose to work with the energy.

June was a pleasant woman, who had a steady job as a doctor's receptionist. She had been divorced several years before and lived a quiet lifestyle, paying rent and running expenses for her cottage from her small salary. It seemed out of character that at certain periods in her life, she should have so many problems because of overspending.

June's natal chart shows a Capricorn Ascendent, with Jupiter in Pisces in the 1st house, squaring the Moon in Sagittarius in the 10th, and squaring Mercury in Gemini in the 4th. Saturn is in the 2nd house in Aries and semi-squares Jupiter. She explained that whenever she was unhappy, she would lose control and spend her rent or electric money to buy something—either that she didn't need or that was for someone else—and then worry because she couldn't pay her bills. Her reaction to most problems usually followed this pattern.

June admitted she was trying to buy herself happiness, but this only aggravated her fundamental problems and made her more unhappy. She needed to look at the root cause of her unhappiness that lay within herself.

She agreed to work with the Saturn Meditation, even though she didn't have a very inspiring picture of the god, but when she realized she could work this way to understand and transform her unhappiness and inadequacies, she became very anxious to begin. Through working with the meditation, June realized that she has always overcompensated with generosity, promises, even self-indulgence, to combat a feeling of being oppressed and inadequate. She has now started to see herself in a new way and has lost many of her old fears and despondencies. This new vision helped her to re-evaluate her way of meeting problems, and she has worked hard to overcome her many anxieties regarding her responsibility to others.

All the personal planets need careful consideration, and by learning to work with them—within the framework of the Meditation—we can bring understanding into the dark areas of our own minds. We can begin to distinguish the true from the false, the real from the unreal, in the gentlest possible way. We can begin to see how we feel when we exchange our weaknesses, fears, and limitations for true strength and understanding, and look at ourselves with kindness that comes from our self-knowledge and awareness. We start to recognize that the pain and suffering we experience is only there through our own ignorance.

> Saturn. This planet applies the tests and is so chosen or invoked because the third ray is not only its particular ray but is also the ray of our planet, the earth. The two notes synchronise. Saturn is also the hierarchical ruler of Libra and, therefore, it brings to the manifestation of mankind and to the various hierarchies

> involved, a point of crisis to which the clue and the outcome lies in the recognition of *balance*. [21]

Saturn's destructive quality should not be underestimated, but to sit back in self-pity and allow lethargy to wash over us is not the answer. It would be impossible to change our lives overnight, but if transits and progressions are causing difficulties, why not use the energy for constructive rather than destructive use?

Do not be fooled by what is holding you back. Is it really Saturn—or is it the confusing deception of Neptune, the indulgence or apparent easy way out of Jupiter, the power-hungry quality of Pluto, the abrasive, freedom-oriented nature of Uranus, or any other difficulty from a personal planet or point in the chart? Think carefully before making your choice.

USING THE SATURN ENERGY TO MAKE DECISIONS

It is certainly true that the more healthy and whole we are, psychologically speaking, the easier it is to make decisions that are not governed by deep inner forces over which we have no control.

> The well-known saying, "The road to hell is paved with good intentions," can be taken in two senses. The first and more obvious one refers to the inertia and weakness of so many good people...The other meaning refers to the bad consequences that can follow acts that are committed with the best of intentions but with little wisdom. [22]

Individual personalities are varied and different, and although some natures may appear friendly and able to respond to others in a loving and spontaneous fashion, this may only be a mask for other problems which perhaps have not been acknowledged and will emerge sooner or later. Without doubt, we all experience problems within relationships, although the problems can assume many different forms. We are all affected by

---

[21] Alice A. Bailey, *Esoteric Astrology* (Albany, NY: Lucis Press, Ltd, 1965), Vol. 3, p. 550.
[22] Roberto Assagioli, *The Act of Will* (New York: Penguin, 1974), p. 154.

unconscious forces, forces that are beyond our control, until we recognize and accept them as our own. Menninger pinpoints one of these unseen influences:

> Love is impaired less by the feeling that we are not appreciated than by a dread, more or less dimly felt by everyone, lest others see through our masks, the masks of repression that have been forced upon us by convention and culture. It is this that leads us to shun intimacy, to maintain friendships on a superficial level, to underestimate and fail to appreciate others lest they come to appreciate us too well.[23]

It is necessary to reach beyond our masks to see ourselves more clearly, so that we are no longer relating solely through defense of ourselves. This defense can operate in so many ways depending on our nature; in learning to like and love our fellow humans, a valuable lesson must be learnt—we must like and love ourselves first, then our response to others can contain more tolerance and sympathy than before.

• • •

When Jason was in his mid 30s he joined a small "enlightened" household in Cambridge. He settled in with his girlfriend of seven years and with ten other people. They spoke about love and harmony, and lived a happy communal life style, which included many spiritual teachings. This lifestyle lasted for several months then Jason found his "universal love" sorely tested; his landlord and teacher decided that he wanted to sleep with Jason's girlfriend. She had made it clear she would agree to this but it was Jason's choice, they said. Jason was faced with a dilemma: should he practice his brotherly principles and let her go, or should he exercise his power and refuse? He chose to let her go—and promptly had a nervous breakdown. He had failed to realize that his spiritual enlightenment was just a mask: the real Jason needed something more, but, by then, it was too late. If he had known himself better he would have had a choice; as it was, he was reacting through false pride and his fear of using power over others. He came for therapy after the event—confused, discouraged, and depressed.

---

[23] Karl Menninger, *Love Against Hate* (San Diego: Harcourt Brace Jovanovich, 1959), p. 22.

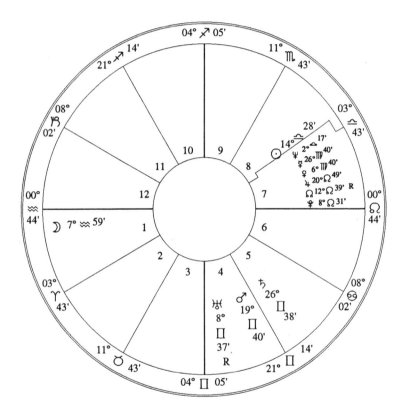

Chart 8. Jason. Birth data from family has been withheld for confidentiality. Chart calculated with Placidus Houses, using Nova/Printwheels.

Jason has five planets and the North Node in the 7th house, showing that many of life's lessons involve others. See Chart 8. His chart shows Mercury conjunct Neptune in Libra in the 7th indicating an idealistic conception of others that could also manifest as confusion in relationships. This conjunction squared Saturn in Gemini in the 5th. This placement seemed to block the love and affection he desired to give and receive from others. Venus in Virgo in the 7th quintiled Saturn and squared Uranus in Gemini in the 4th, showing perhaps some sense of dissatisfaction with the home life perhaps manifesting in the situation with his girlfriend. Relationship decisions made suddenly without forethought are indicated, although the quintile could have balanced some of this. Pluto in the 7th in Leo conjuncts the North Node, indicating power struggles and manipulation from others who seem to be the strong ones. The conjunction of Pluto to the North Node forces Jason to transform through others. Pluto sextiles Neptune and Uranus—the power can be Jason's power—and bestows much wisdom and ability for transformation if accepted. Jupiter in Leo is also in the 7th conjuncting the North Node, so he must have received pleasure through others, although there was the danger of letting others take on the role of the wise teacher. Jason's Sun is in Libra in the 8th trine the Moon, Mars, and Uranus, and sextile Jupiter, Pluto and the North Node. Here was his salvation. After working with the natal chart for a few sessions, he took the problem to Saturn.

The journey was quite easy; I was anxious to get there as I needed help. I was confused. I had tried to do what I thought best but to no avail. The gift I take to Saturn is a stone Janus head, representing my present confusion. This confusion arises out of what I should do—what I should seek to do now. What should my attitude be to others—teachers, fellow searchers, who seem in command? What should my attitude be to those who try to manipulate me? And is it possible to proceed, as I wish, without using power over others?

The gatekeeper is an amiable, quiet man of some depth. He nods and lets me in. The first thing that strikes me inside is that they are all taller than I am, which is unexpected. There is a large crowd. I recognize some of the faces—they are friends and relatives. There's a very heavy feel.

At this point, I feel too tired to get into this. I walk through them feeling uneasy—not threatened—uneasy, as if I know something I don't want to know. I walk towards Saturn.

There are so many people, it is as if they are dragging me down. As I clear the crowd and cross the open space towards Saturn, the sensation goes. It is a long way to Saturn. His throne is in a recess raised by three steps. He is very young and agile looking. His right arm hangs over the arm rest, his index finger touching the top of an hourglass, with the sand in the upper part.

His left hand in his lap is closed over a golden orb. He has auburn hair encircled by a golden crown. He looks at me—giving me a feeling of radiant hope. I feel heavy and old in comparison with him! I like him. I give him the Janus head saying it represents my confused state.

He leans forward to take it lovingly in both hands, looking at it from many angles, stroking the stone. He smiles, looking for a place to put it, seemingly cannot decide, and goes to hand it back—as if to say, "This is your problem"—and then places it in his lap with the orb on top, using his left hand.

He says, "And so what should your attitude be to your Self? You are the boundary and extent. Your place is your Self. In this place you need no attitude—you are and you follow your Self. Let others find their own path—without your help—do not hinder, but do not help. Be there.

"It is what your life is about: being there. Under what obligation are you other than to be your Self—trust it. It, after all, is you. It is the crossroads, the center. Through it, all pass, all come, all go. All gain entry, or not. It is the weighbridge of experience— life's coming and going. Truth sees.

"I know your concern. I know your fear. Can you be manipulated when the Self is there? Speak.

"No—always no. Others cannot live your life for you. You do what your Self wishes—that's all. Yes it is hard. Learn.

"Fear and illusions grip us.... Truth loosens the grip. Desire strengthens it—And desire has many forms. Beware spiritual searching's glamorous snare. And always, and in everything, try and relate through Self. Also Self to Self, and not person to person.

"Keep the inward center turning. Like a lighthouse, its beam revealing. Trust—learn to trust this Self. It is your font, your cup, your grail. In it—is all. And all is clear."

At this point I think with relief, "No more searching up blind alleys. Now the Self."

I become Saturn. The golden orb feels warm. The energy is high and light. There is a limitless feeling of time and energy, of clarity, hope, and intelligence. I look at Jason, seeing an aged careworn figure, perplexed and unsure, tired and almost at the end—soon the Self will come.

I would like to give him hope and courage—for his last gasps of the old self, to ease the butterfly out of the chrysalis. I give him a golden key saying, "This is your talisman."

I see the others there standing as in a wake—uneasy, uncomfortable full of forboding. Wondering where they will go. Ghosts—to dissolve in the light.

Let them go and become their true selves. I feel ascendance—lightness and energy—I am full of both.

I become Jason again. I thank Saturn and he says, "Come often and soon."

He is bigger than he was, with more stature, authority, and maturity.

As I walk through the crowds they turn their heads not wanting to meet my eyes.

I wonder why and hear, "We are not that we seem."

The gatekeeper is the same.

This was Jason's story. There are many people like Jason who are afraid of power for they do not realize true power is from the Self. These people find it hard to say no to others—they feel often that to say no is not a charitable thing to do. This often occurs at the expense of themselves and personal relationships.

• • •

Kate was one such person. She worked as a nurse, was also a wife, mother, and grandmother. She was the sort of person everyone used: she did the unpopular shifts on the wards, rushed home to feed and clean the family, and help with the young grandchildren, ran jumble sales, collected money for the dog's home, and visited sick and elderly people. She gave no time to herself, was always tired, and did not have time to eat properly. By the time Kate was in her late 40s she was internally angry, miserable, and depressed. She hardly spoke to her husband and had no friends she could turn to for support. It was only when Kate sought therapy to untangle her mixed-up emotions that she began to realize why she was so unhappy.

Kate has Sun in Gemini in the 8th squaring Neptune in Virgo in the 11th (see Chart 9), perhaps showing a misguided sense of duty to the group and a mistaken idea of others' needs and values. She has a Scorpio Ascendant and Moon which she apparently had never accepted, as she was thought of by others as a "good sort" and good sorts do not feel jealous, angry, and resentful. The Scorpio Moon in the 1st opposes Saturn and Jupiter in Taurus in the 7th, indicating her feeling of emotional separation from others, yet there is also a need to open emotionally. The Moon, however, rules the 9th house which contains Venus, Mercury, and Mars in Cancer, all of which sextile the Moon, Saturn, and Jupiter.

While in therapy, Kate found out many things about herself—she found that she couldn't live others' lives for them—and what was right for some was not right for others. This included members of her own family. She realized she had tried to give everyone what she thought they wanted rather than what they did want. She became very discouraged at this point, feeling her whole life had been wasted, but she agreed to continue. She came to the conclusion that she had a right to choose her own way, that she was as deserving of attention as others, she deserved some time to do things. At this point she wrote the following.

I am lost in a muddle. I must stand up and be counted.
    I have to live my life and let others live theirs.
Help where I can but not at the expense of my own happiness.
    I'm me and I count.
I can't keep lying down and letting everyone walk all over me.
    I can't keep giving when there is nothing else to give.
I can only do the best I can.
    I must be stronger and live my own life.

The problem was taken to Saturn. This is the first visit.

The Hall is dark and cold; no people there; Saturn wears a dark cloak. He is very hawk-like; dark tanned skin; long dark hair. I feel frightened. I give Saturn a rock—which he throws aside.

I say, "I want to know you but I am frightened."

He seems a little more approachable. "Why?" he replies.

I tell him it is because I need his love and want to love him. He takes my hand—he is so big and cold-looking—but his hands are warm.

I become Saturn—and feel very powerful. I see Kate as very insignificant. There are lots of people there waiting for orders. My every wish is fulfilled by the people. Kate is very stupid and weak. I give her a sword that she cannot lift, telling her she must find her own way down the mountain.

I become Kate again. I am feeling very angry with Saturn—he is laughing at me—I am determined to get the sword down the mountain—with or without his help. He shouts, "Be strong."

Kate had a second visit to Saturn which went as follows.

I take the sword back to Saturn—he says "Keep it." I feel pleased to see him. The people there are happy today. The hall is brightly lit—warm and comfortable.

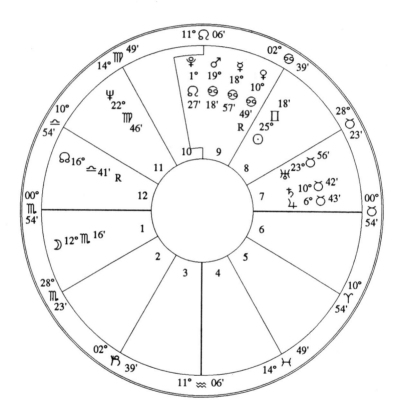

Chart 9. Kate. Birth data from family has been withheld for confidentiality. Chart calculated with Placidus Houses, using Nova/Printwheels.

Saturn is pleased to see me—he likes me, I know. He gives me a staff—to help me keep strong and upright when the going is rough.

I become Saturn—and feel very strong. I say to Kate, "*You* must have faith in yourself. *You* must be strong."

I see she is not so afraid of everybody now. She looks pleased and happy—warm and glowing.

I am Kate again. Saturn says, "Walk tall with your head up—you must have trust—trust before distrust. You try and manage everything and everybody because you are afraid of being hurt. You hold everything in. Take the wall down between you and others—*instead* of looking over it. The wall keeps people out and yourself in—it grew through fear. Fear of life—people—not being good enough. To get the wall down trust in your Self. Let go of the past—live for the future. Stop looking back. Stop judging everything from past experiences. Accept NOW."

Kate found that by working with and understanding the Saturn placement in her chart, she began to learn to recognize what was causing her interrelationships to be less than perfect. It is obvious none of us can relate "wholly" when we are relating to others through our masks of repression, which are woven together from past fears as well as the social grouping which we call our own. These fears inevitably feed the need for defense which alienates us from others and renders us more isolated and lonely.

• • •

Such apprehensions and fears can also be projected onto a section of society, a race, or religion. Contemporary and past atrocities are the products of national fear and the philosophy of "an eye for an eye" can only feed the negativity and trigger off a negative force in the world. This force will continue to have effect until the energy is turned to a more positive use to benefit humanity, and this can only be achieved by understanding.

The following extract is by a man who went through four years with the Underground Movement in occupied France in the Second World War.

All victories are ephemeral and revenge only breeds revenge, generating an endless vicious cycle. Yet war has broadened my vision. False concepts have been replaced by perception of an acuteness sometimes resented by others. Yet my new outlook was located in a dichotomy which filled me with disillusion. The behavior of the Victors at every level was far different from what I had naively hoped. False decisions and their consequences set in motion a new cycle of error, little different from the pre-war world. It made me think it is impossible to leave the beaten track—another cause for despondency. Only years later did I fully understand the psychological revolution needed to make a real change possible.[24]

So, if we are defensive because of some deep insecurity or fear, this will be triggered off again and again by circumstances—unless we choose to understand and work with it. Thus, we come back again to choice. It is necessary to be as honest and true to ourselves as possible because so many decisions we make concern others as well as ourselves. There must be different ways of approaching decisions: some inner compulsions, as already shown, make us no more than puppets pulled by strings on the stage of life. If this is the case, there is no free will at all. Francis Wickes says:

Refusal of inward choice and its creative power makes of life a repetitious round, a treadmill of duty or a merry-go-round of meaningless activity. Man is bound to the wheel of fate until consciousness of his God-given power of choice dawns on him. Then he glimpses the paradoxical nature of the force that has both bound him and given him the power to break the bonds if he will choose the pain entailed in the struggle and accept the perils of freedom to be encountered on the spiral way that sweeps upward from the broken wheel.[25]

If we can understand ourselves better, we can relate to others through a truer choice, rather than with a negative response arising from some inner

[24] Frederic Lionel, *Challenge* (Essex: United Kingdom, 1980), pp. 134, 135.
[25] Frances Wickes, *The Inner World of Choice*, pp. 2, 3..

defense mechanism. Then those choices and decisions, honest and freely given, will be of greater discernment than any that are motivated by unknown forces of one sort or another.

How does one make a decision that is free and unafraid? Learn to understand what the Saturn energy entails, look deep within your heart at your own inner fears and insecurities, while recognizing Saturn's positive structure within your life and the need for certain boundaries and restrictions. Take these and work with the Meditation and be unafraid to search the deepest corners of your nature. The more you can do this, the nearer you will come to being able to use free will based on a fair judgment of the situation.

The Saturn Meditation

When I have given lectures or taken workshops showing people how to work with their Saturn energy, there seems to have been great interest in and positive use of the suggested techniques. The lectures have always been to astrology groups, but the workshops have included many people with no knowledge of astrology at all, just an interest in self-awareness and growth.

These exercises have something to offer people who want to understand why they feel as they do, why there seem to be areas full of failure and frustration in their lives. Through trying to understand why they suffer oppression, limitation, depression, jealousy, or inferiority, they can change their way of thinking and transform their lives *if they so choose.*

By working with the exercise, you can understand and change areas of life where things have not worked in the past. It is important that, as you work, you keep a notebook so that nothing is lost. This can benefit you enormously.

Perhaps you have problems with relationships. Are you happy as you are? It is your choice: you may decide to stay as you are—or you may like to look at the problem from a new angle. Start working through whatever seems to be blocking you. Often it appears that we are being opposed by a situation or person outside ourselves. But these are usually projections of our own.

You may choose to reject this theory or you may decide to work with the difficulties. It is always your choice. It has been said that there is no such thing as a problem that doesn't bring a gift for you in the long run. We want to find the gift, and the following list will summarize the various benefits and experiences you may have while working with the Saturn Meditation technique.

1) During heavy Saturn transits or progressions, it is advisable to use the meditation as often as is needed, for example, once a week or more if required. Sometimes you may go weeks without using it but you will know it is always there when you need it.

2) If you cannot visualize easily, just imagine or "feel" the experience as you would in a daydream. Take the first images that come to mind, do not try to change them, and remember—the more you practice, the easier the flow and exchange from the unconscious will be.

3) The *land* you find yourself in, and your journey, signify the difficulties we all experience at certain times in life. It is, in fact, setting the scene for meeting the God. Climbing the mountain, symbolizes that you are climbing towards the spiritual or highest interpretation of the Saturn energy.

4) The *gatekeeper* is the part of you that allows you to meet the God within. Often, at the start, he can be mistrustful of you and your motives for being there. When he asks you what you want, you have to give him an answer that satisfies him before he will let you in.

5) Most people experience *the people in the hall* as they would in life. It often accentuates the negative element. The image can also be affected by transits or progressions occurring at that time.

6) When you give your *gift* to Saturn it can be something you ask him to accept that you do not need anymore (e.g., some condition or state of mind such as fears or pride). It is a good idea to imagine giving them to him tied in a sack. You can give some project or area of growth—if you share with him good things, in return, you'll receive his strength to continue. You could also give a symbolic gift that you may not understand. (You may not understand it consciously if it comes directly from the unconscious.) However, it needs to be noted as it may be understood days, or even weeks, later.

7) When you become the *God*, you are experiencing the positive effect of the Saturn energy. You can realize that you have something to offer from your own experiences of life.

8) Saturn's gift can be something to help us or something that gives us a vision of the future. It is often symbolic and so needs to be noted. It may be understood at the time or later.

9)   This way of working is like having a therapist or guru who is wise and all-knowing at one's call the whole time. By working this way, many can learn to develop that which is the only source of true peace and wholeness. Obviously there are many who do this in their own way, but all who ask for help using this meditation, receive according to their own needs.

10) To do the meditation, sit or lie down in a comfortable position and thoroughly relax.

11) You can make notes at different points throughout the meditation or wait until the meditation has finished. When doing the meditation, I use a cassette tape and pause it at the different points of interchange, writing notes at the time—but everyone should find the way that is easiest and the most convenient for them.

AN EXAMPLE OF SATURN MEDITATION

Imagine a very cold country.
The landscape is bleak—barren.
The sky is gray—there's a cold icy mist.
And there are dark forbidding mountains in the distance.

You feel cold and shivery
Heavy and tired.
There's no one there—it's lonely and cold.
An icy wind whips around you.
Your body aches—you feel tired and weary
But you walk onward toward the mountains.

As you get nearer to the mountains
You see snow in patches on them
And mist around their craggy peaks.

You walk on for some time
And eventually reach the lower slopes of the mountains.
Now there are boulders on the path—the way is difficult
But you persevere.
You feel so cold and lonely
You press on.

You walk on for some time and eventually reach the lower slopes of the mountains. Now there are boulders on the path—the way is difficult.

You climb over stones
And edge your way around boulders.
Now you see a path that leads up
To the huge gray cold mountain.
You start to climb,
Your legs ache—and the air is getting colder.

Stop and look below—notice how high you have climbed.
Continue, even though you are weary.

Now you walk into a thick cold mist—you cannot see.
Just edge forward inch by inch.
You may trip and fall—feel your way with your hands.
You struggle through the mist—not knowing where you are
Or where you are going.
You continue feeling lonely and lost.
The mist thins.
You see a huge plateau.
There is still a lot of mist.

Rising from the mist is a huge black stone temple.
This is the place you wanted to find.

You walk to the door—the sky seems darker.
Knock on the door—which is opened by the gatekeeper.
What does he look like?—what is he wearing?
How do you feel about him?

He will ask you what you want.
Tell him why you are there—why you want to see Saturn.
He may answer—or he may just let you in.

When inside, you are shown into a huge hall—
there are people there.
The ceilings are high—the hall long.
Look at the people—what they wear—how they are behaving.
How do you feel about them?

At the other end of the hall you see a huge stone throne.
There is a large figure on the throne.

You see a huge plateau. There is still a lot of mist. Rising from the mist is a huge black stone temple. This is the place you wanted to find.

It is Saturn—the God Kronos.
Walk toward him.
Look up at him—
Notice how he sits—
how he holds his arms and hands.
Can you see what he wears?
Can you see his face?
Does he have anything on his head—
What is his hair like?
How does he make you feel?

Ask him if he will work with you and be your friend.
Tell him why you're there—what you want.
How you want him to help you.
Give him the gift you have brought for him.
It may be anything—it may be symbolic.
Does he accept it?

Ask him anything else you may wish to—
and listen to his reply.

Notice how you feel.

Now imagine walking out of your own body—
And walking into the body of Saturn.
You become the God sitting on his throne.
You take on his shape and form.
Feel yourself in his body—looking out of his eyes at you.

How do you see yourself—do you like what you see?
How do you see the others in the hall?—
some you may know.

Give a gift to the person in front of you
Who has come to ask your help.
How can you help this person on their journey?

As you sit on the throne feel your strength—
Your responsibility.

Feel your power and ability to help the person in front of you—
And the others in the hall.
Realize what you are feeling is your own energy—
your own strength.
And anytime you choose you can experience this feeling.
For a moment or two, experience taking on your full power—
Using your full positive Saturn energy.

Note how you feel.

After experiencing this energy,
Step back out of the God
And back into your own body—
Become you again.
When this is done turn and look at Saturn.
Is he different?—Do you feel any different?

Thank him for seeing you.
Ask if you may come back to see him
and "speak" to him again.
If you wish to say any final words to him do so—
And listen to any reply.

When you have finished say Good-bye.

Walk down the hall to the door.
Is the gatekeeper the same—or has he changed?
How do you feel about him?

Walk outside.
Perhaps the Sun is starting to shine.
And the clouds are moving away.

Walk across the plateau
And take the path down the mountain.
The mist is almost gone.
As you walk down you may see tiny flowers
Starting to blossom in the rock's crevices.

The long long winter is nearly over.

Walk down the mountain.
As you walk down
Let your consciousness come back into your own room.
And open your eyes.

Part II

SUBPERSONALITIES

Subpersonalities are psychological satellites, coexisting as a multitude of lives within the overall medium of our personality. Each subpersonality has a style and motivation of its own, often strikingly dissimilar from those of the others. Says the Portuguese poet Fernando Pessoa, "In every corner of my soul there is an altar to a different god."

—————*Piero Ferrucci*

Subpersonalities and Astrology

In the Introduction, we discussed subpersonalities. What are they? How do they work in our lives? How do they fit in with the natal chart and astrological viewpoints? Figure 2 (page 90) illustrates in a simple way how the different energies within the natal chart form divergent parts of our personality, including particular and differing character traits. Some of these unite and work together within the personality; others are alienated and pushed out. In some cases a very dominant subpersonality will take over almost entirely, usually smothering more positive personality traits.

Two symbolic figures from *The Wizard of Oz,* who turn up time and time again when one works with the subpersonality meditation, are Aquarians with the Tin Man who cannot cry and who is looking for a heart and Leos with the Frightened Lion. Other common symbols are the Martyr, which is often signified in the chart by a strong Neptune or Piscean influence. There is also the Victim, often connected to Saturn in Aries or in the first house, although severe manifestations often require a hard aspect from Neptune as well. Then there are the Dictator and the Hater or Hag, which are often although not always strongly Plutonian or Scorpionic.

It should be remembered that any subpersonality, whatever its nature, is only a *part* of the individual personality; but if not allowed to express itself and develop, it will at times cause disturbances within the psyche. Sometimes these disturbances will be severe, in some cases causing mental breakdown and physical illness. Always remember this dominance can take many forms—it is just as common in the Martyr and Victim type of subpersonality as it is in any more dictatorial form (see the section entitled "Subpersonalities and Saturn").

There are many different and varied subpersonalities. No one planetary influence is responsible in making up these characters. Piero Ferrucci speaks of them in relation to the archetypes.

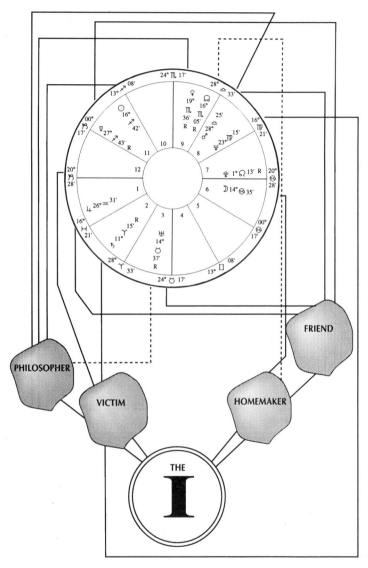

Figure 2. Particular astrological energies, illustrated by Joan Smith's natal chart, directly relate to the subpersonalities that are part of her personality. Birth data has been withheld for confidentiality. Chart has been calculated with Placidus Houses, using Nova/Printwheels.

Subpersonalities are like exiled gods—caricatures, degraded specimens of the original, luminous archetypes. But there is a difference: while there seems to be little hope for the exiled gods (in Heine's poetical vision, at any rate), subpersonalities are clearly susceptible to transformation. Instead of degraded archetypes, they can be regarded as psychological contents striving to emulate an archetype, as a gross version of what is to appear later in a much more refined form.[1]

Certain signs often show a similarity of archetypal image. Taureans, or those with planets in Taurus, often have a figure that loves the country; it can be a country housewife, a gardener, a gypsy, or some other rural figure. Sun or planets in Cancer obviously often have a mother image, or a figure who loves his or her home, as in the hostess, the lady of the manor, the cook, the housekeeper, or some other similar character. The list is varied and no set rules can be laid down from the natal chart alone, or from any one planetary position as to what kind of subpersonalities we may develop. Understanding ourselves and our subpersonalities can only come through working on an inner level with each personality. By doing this, we tap into and become that individual part—experiencing its needs and desires, identifying where it fits into our lives. People are often surprised by what they find when working this way. It is a valuable and enlightening exercise, one that can lay the foundation for understanding ourselves better.

It is important when discussing subpersonalities to try to realize how we relate to others through these elements. Some people bring out the better part of our natures, some the worst. If we begin to understand all parts of our diverse character, we can start to recognize why we react as we do in different circumstances and with different people. Sometimes it seems the worse we feel, the more we chase the elusive butterfly that we call happiness. Do we only feel good when life, other people, circumstances, and conditions are going our way? What about the other 90 percent of the time? What do we do then—wish for a distant dream of everything turning out right? This attitude can often make things worse. How do we go about improving present conditions?

---

[1] Piero Ferrucci, *What We May Be* (London: Crucible, 1989), p. 55.

It is often a surprise to discover that the person we thought we were was just a figment of our imagination, and if this is so, who are we? Am I the part of myself that is confident or the part of myself that is inferior? Am I the part of myself that loves to play and take the easy way out, or am I the hard-working Martyr? Am I the part of myself that lets others take advantage of me or the active aggressor? And if I am not these—again who am I?

Now it seems reasonable to assume that the lower nature is only our manifestation for this lifetime—so it makes sense to try to understand how we work, what we consist of. How can we do this? First we have to learn to understand ourselves with the mind; this can be done through a thorough understanding of the natal chart. Then by working on an inner level with the subpersonalities, we begin to understand ourselves on the deepest levels, moving from unconscious actions to conscious choices—using Saturn to help us achieve more responsibility and balance in those choices. Without the responsibility and insight from Saturn, no genuine choices can be made. Finally, by working with Pluto, we look into those dark areas of our minds to transform and let go of those influences that we no longer require, and allow in their place a new consciousness to be born.

We need to understand and work with every part of our personality. The more we try to avoid or suppress something we do not like within ourselves, the more this part of us will cry for attention. When people get to know their subpersonalities, and the parts that go to make them up, then they can begin to develop greater harmony and unity within themselves— thus bringing greater unity and harmony without. They can develop a dialogue within, have a meeting of subpersonalities to make sure all parts of their natures are being heard. In the way a company would have a board meeting, we can do the same thing only on an inner level. Once the differing parts of our nature have been identified, we can begin to make sure all parts are acknowledged, accepted, integrated, and synthesized.

• • •

Eric came for therapy after suffering a mental breakdown from overwork at age 40. He had achieved a high position in his career, but at the expense of his peace of mind and of any personal enjoyment at work or at home. He felt utterly trapped by his lifestyle and had to work harder and harder to maintain the status quo. He has a Cancer Sun and Ascendant, with Mars conjunct Pluto in Leo in the 1st house, Saturn in Taurus on the cusp between the 10th and 11th houses. His subpersonalities were a Large Bossy Woman in her 60s, possessive and jealous of youth, a Shy Teenage Girl, a Small Boy, and a Lion. At the beginning of therapy he describes meeting two of his subpersonalities.

> I met a young child I liked very much, he was happy and carefree: he made me feel rather awkward and formal, as though I would like to get out of my stiff suit and play with him. Then I met a very shabby-looking lion: his coat was moth-eaten, and he looked old and baggy as though his skin didn't fit him properly. I thought he looked very comical as he stood on his hind legs as though he wanted to be a man. He seemed very shy and nervous, and when I said "Hello," he covered himself as though for protection. I went into and became this Lion personality; I felt shy, awkward, ill at ease, very vulnerable as a male, as I felt all the younger stronger lions were out to take my place. I observed my outer self; I looked confident and young, and I thought, 'I want to be strong like him.' I tried to make myself into a strong, young male lion, and started pacing up and down. I really felt I was becoming younger and stronger as I did this. Then the young child I had met earlier ran up to me and said, 'Hello nice lion, will you come and play with me?' The child was very happy and innocent. I moved back into my outer self again, watching the young boy playing with the lion, which was again a rather comical figure. I then had a vision of what the comical lion would do if he became the strong, young male lion—he would kill the child.

How many times had this happened before, when Eric's own inner child had said "Let's play?" His fear was that if he played with this innocent child, he would kill or hurt it in some way. During therapy he also discovered there was a fear that this child would grow up and be a threat to him—as other young males were. He was in the position of being completely impotent, for to acknowledge the child—who symbolized play and relaxation—implied a threat, but to ignore it brought even greater anguish. As he learned to work with and understand these two personalities within himself, his outer projections started to change. He found he could delegate much of his work to the younger staff—without the fear they would take him over. In fact, in time, he began to really enjoy helping the younger members of the group. They appreciated this, and his fear of being dethroned receded into the past—plus he had much more time to take up outside interests and he began to learn how to "play." He realized that any threat he had felt came only through his own insecurities.

If the ego lets the desires rule, it finds itself pulled by its lower nature, but it can learn to use these desires in the service of the Universal Self. Then, and only then, is the lower will joined with the higher will. The strength or weakness of the ego's energy is derived from the Sun, its sign, house and, most important, its aspects. In *The Art of Synthesis,* Alan Leo describes the ego as the feeling of "I," and says the Sun represents universal life when referring to the living body, just as it represents universal consciousness when referring to the soul.[2] Esoteric philosophy teaches the existence of two egos: the mortal or personal, and the divine and impersonal. Sometimes the personal ego is referred to as the self and the impersonal and divine ego as the Self.

The feeling of "I" when attached to the Universal or Soul principle is not the normal "I" that may think or boast: Look what I have done. Look what power I have over others. Aren't I good! I've got it right. Look at all the possessions I own. Look how much I help others. Or even, I have found the right religion. Only the mortal, corporal self attached to the personal will would think this way. There is no suggestion implied here that the human part of ourselves is undesirable. On the contrary, it comprises many experiences formed from past needs and desires, which are made up from previous lives and are necessary in the natural evolution of ourselves and our universe.

If we consider the mortal part unwelcome and unwanted, we are acting under the impulse from the human self. The Spiritual or Higher Self, if strong enough, looks upon weaknesses from its own human nature with great compassion and kindness, much like a loving parent looks upon a

---

[2] Alan Leo, *The Art of Synthesis*, p. 260.

child. We need to remember we are human, and in understanding our human nature, we become more "Self" conscious, which brings liberation and the developing awareness of our own divine heritage.

Therefore, if we compare this personal ego or "I," with the ego or "I" connected to the Soul, it is like comparing the luminosity of a light bulb to the Sun's brilliance and light in the heavens.

Difficulties which have not been worked through are often caused by hard aspects to the Sun—our ego—and affect us by causing the "I" to undergo a shift. When this shift occurs, the person involved has no power to detach from the subpersonalities as depicted by the lower nature. Until the ego can learn to assume its rightful place—at the intermediary point between the human nature, made from the planetary energies, and the Soul Principle—it has no power of choice or free will but is pulled hither and thither by its own uncontrollable desires.

Someone with a hard aspect from Pluto to the Sun may feel uncon- sciously coerced to be obsessive and controlling, due to some hidden defense mechanism—thus the center shifts and is no longer the center because any energy from this planet is using the ego rather than being used by it. However, anyone with this planetary configuration can learn how to use the transforming energy of Pluto to achieve greater awareness. To do this means reading and re-reading, understanding and re-understanding what the particular aspect of Pluto to the Sun signifies in that particular chart—and what it signifies in that person's life. It is necessary also to trace sign, house position, and other aspects to Pluto. The more conscious we become, the less unconsciously are we controlled.

A difficult aspect from Neptune to the Sun causes confusion and fear—a feeling of not being able to trust the Self. This type of person can just muddle through life—not trusting people they should and trusting some they perhaps shouldn't. This trust, or sometimes distrust, is not always connected to other people: sometimes it is connected to a cause, a religion, a way of life. In fact, it can encompass many things, and so its "real" significance must be looked for carefully. Neptune's sign, house place- ment, and other aspects need careful analysis, for as with other difficult aspects to the Sun, this throws the "I" or Ego off balance. Thus, the Self's real energy cannot manifest. The positive use of this energy is in under- standing the more subtle vibrations of a mystical nature—realizing there is a truth beyond words, a truth that can be felt—although never truly expressed other than within or through the Self.

The same applies to Uranus in hard aspect to the Sun, often causing an unnecessary need for freedom or to be different, thus never working through anything properly and missing developing any real strength from the Self. The positive use of this energy is the ability to use the insight, inventiveness, and sudden flashes of cognition received from Uranus in service to one's self and others.

As with other planets, Saturn can distort the ego's energy when in hard aspect to the Sun, causing a lack of self-worth, a feeling of limitation connected to the signs Saturn and the Sun are in. There is often a self-denying element here, and again, until investigated and worked with, this will cause our center to distort. Jupiter in hard aspect to the Sun causes some difficulty in the relating principle, often with an inability to recognize the real needs of the self. Another dilemma is connected to Mars in hard aspect to the Sun: it causes anger, an attitude of "it's not fair," expressed consciously or unconsciously. So the Self's energy is again blocked, the center distorted. All hard aspects to the Sun need careful analysis and investigation, including those connected to the Mid-heaven, Ascendant, and North Node. Once this is done, we really are stepping off the wheel of fate and using the God-given power of choice. We do at last begin to see the nature of the force that has bound us and given us the power to break the bonds if we so choose, and in Frances Wickes' words, ". . .accept the perils of freedom to be encountered on the spiral way that sweeps upward from the broken wheel."[3]

---

[3] Frances Wickes, *The Inner World of Choice*, p. 3.

Subpersonalities and Saturn

Joan Smith, who has briefly been introduced in chapter one, came for therapy because of severe depression. She explained, with difficulty, how she had a problem communicating with people and expressing her thoughts. This, she said, caused her to be very isolated and lonely. She had been seeing another psychotherapist weekly for six months and this therapist used the method of silence to make the patient open up and talk. She said she could not talk, so they just sat there saying nothing. Before this, she had spent four months with another person who was training to be a counselor, and although she was able to talk to her and build up a friendly relationship, the person had told Joan she could not see her anymore, as she felt Joan was becoming abnormally attached to her. Each time, no matter what the circumstances, Joan became the "victim." There seemed to be a pattern in her life, and no matter how hard she tried, everyone she came into contact with eventually undermined her confidence. She explained how, right from early school days to the times when she was a teenager and through two marriages, she was completely unable to express herself and her needs. The result was loneliness, isolation, and finally depression which became worse as time went by.

Joan had been married twice. She met her second husband through a marriage bureau: he was an extremely hard-working man who ran a small but successful business started by his grandfather. He wanted someone to look after his large home in the country and his child from a previous marriage. The house, although very desirable, was situated on its own, a mile from the nearest village with no near neighbors. Joan felt she had no contact with her husband and was just there to provide the meals, keep the house clean, and somehow manage the large and rambling garden. This made her desperately unhappy, and that desperation had led her again to seek therapy. So tense, depressed, confused, and unable to sleep, she had come to seek help. Her marriage had brought her neither security nor reassurance, but at least her husband was sympathetic enough to support her therapy.

From her earliest childhood, she had feelings of doubt and insecurity, doubting her own mind and judgment. She was the middle of three children born to older parents; throughout her childhood, she had felt left out and rejected. Her older sister was very clever, and she had dominated Joan and always ended up having her own way with her parents. Her younger brother was physically and mentally handicapped and took up all their mother's time and energy. Joan had not been strong as a child and had missed schooling through ill health. She said she could remember long hours lying in her bedroom, waiting for her busy mother to come to her, not wanting to make any fuss or bother. This had actually exaggerated her feelings of inadequacy.

As a teenager she again missed schooling through ill health; this also caused her to lose touch with one or two special friends she had managed to make. So, again, she was left alone, unhappy, and without friends. She met her first husband when she was 20, and she described him as "someone like me." But the marriage had not worked: they could neither communicate nor respond to each other; each became more insular and lonely as time went on, and finally they divorced.

Now in her second marriage, the introspection and feeling of frustration had intensified to such a pitch that she genuinely believed she was becoming mentally ill. Her natal chart (see figure 2 on page 90) showed Pluto at 1° Leo in the 7th house, squared by transiting Pluto, showing a need for transformation within her relationships. Uranus was transiting through Sagittarius, her Sun sign, in the 11th house, showing a need for positive change in connection to herself, her aspirations, and her friendships.

Joan had a lot of unrealized potential. She was intuitive, easy to work with, and had strong philosophical tendencies. Also she was keen to learn, but she couldn't protect herself. We worked for many sessions with the natal chart, discussing also the relevance of karma. We spoke of Saturn and the need to accept responsibility for ourselves and all that goes to make ourselves up. Then we started working with the subpersonalities, using the method in the following chapter to communicate with them.

On the subpersonality journey, she easily reached the dwelling place and met and liked The Philosopher—the part of her that enjoyed sharing ideas with others, had many interests, liked traveling, was optimistic and open; The Friend—who enjoyed others company, was open and loyal; The Homemaker—caring, liking security and enjoying entertaining at home. She quickly found and maintained a good dialogue with them all. They in turn liked her and each other; any changes or wants from them were readily accepted and understood by the others. But it was a different matter when she met The Victim—anxiety from childhood, feeling dumb, daft, self-conscious, lacking confidence, isolated as a teenager—all these feelings returned when in a guided meditation the following exchange took place.

Joan saw a thin ragged figure come from the room; he seemed to want to hide and refused at first to go outside. Eventually he did go into the garden, and Joan was asked to describe what she saw. "I see a man, he looks very old, although I think perhaps he is not as old as he looks, he is not very tall, and looks very thin and ill. His face, which he keeps hiding, has large hollow eyes. He reminds me of an old tramp who was about when I was a child. Everyone said he was mad and laughed at and ridiculed him."

She is then asked how she feels about him. "I do not like him, he is nasty, horrible, I do not want to look at him, he is pathetic."

"Why not ask him what he wants?" the therapist asks.

"What do you want?" Joan asks.

"I do not want to be so alone, I want you to be my friend, I want someone to take care of me," replies the Victim.

Joan at this point begins to get upset and refuses to speak to the Victim anymore; she says she will do anything but will not be made more unhappy by having to think that this horrible old tramp is part of herself. She wants to get better but says she cannot do it this way. We agree at the next session to take this problem to Saturn. She also wanted to give Saturn more of her "fears," particularly in connection to the Victim.

Joan's meeting with Saturn is as follows.

Saturn is shining white marble. He is enormous—his big toe is six feet high—I can't see him, all I can see is his knees!

Saturn is shining white marble. He is enormous—his big toe is six feet high—I can't see him, all I can see is his knees! What is it in me that makes you this big, I ask?

"What is it in me that makes you this big," I ask.

"That which wishes to reduce you and rob you of your true place," Saturn replies. He is craning over his knees peering at me. He is reassuring in his attitude—realizing my predicament.

I give him my gift, a bag of fears.

"Put it by my foot," Saturn says. "It is too small for me to take."

I ask my question, "I am composed of different energies that make up certain personalities within me; clearly they will be expressed consciously or otherwise. I wish to be responsible in this and work consciously with them. But it does not seem sensible to surrender or agree to whatever they propose, so how can I. . .?"

"Know that this is why you are here," Saturn replies. I understand.

"It is simpler than you think: just flow *with* (not in)," he continues. At this point I try to explain all the difficulties I have had with the Victim, and how I cannot accept this part of me, and what it wants from me.

Saturn says, "Ask him again what he wants. Have regard. Have regard. Do not do *what* he wants. But have regard for what he wants. Perhaps he does not want what you *think* he wants. Have regard. Experience all his wants. Perhaps he wants more acknowledgment and positive recognition. Perhaps he wants more dialogue—dialogue with you—as you want dialogue with me. So much terror, so much fear, over something in essence that is very simple.

"You say 'yes,' or you say 'no'; you say 'let's talk.' How do you control horses? You lead them where you want them to go. Or—let them take you where they want to go. These energies are not mindless, nor stupid—*talk* to them. They are living presences who wish to show you something. Does he really want your acquiescence? Or your liberty? Talk to him. Find out."

I become Saturn, I see Joan as agitated. There is no one else there, just piles of dust. I suddenly realize karma is simple—it has to be worked out—like a seam of ore.

I give Joan a crystal ball—for guidance—for clear vision. I feel Saturn's strength and lawful rigidity—the necessity of confinement—and boundaries.

I become Joan again and look up at Saturn. He has returned to human size. And I understand the positive merit of restriction.

Joan then asked Saturn what actually should her relationship with the Victim be.

"Your relationship with the Victim needs to be one of identification or de-identification—at the moment it is one of rejection. It needs to become acceptance. See the Victim being on equal footing with the others. Assume responsibility, first to accept; then promote; then understand him:—for he is also a facet of yourself—the mental clothing that you are obliged to have. Maybe mental body is truer—the mental as opposed to the physical covering.

"They are all your symptoms. They are complexes, thought forms, which embody traits—accepted (all the others), or rejected (the Victim). They are your make up but not you. They are your living mask—the necessary form that you need (karmically) to take.

"They are you (mentally) as your body (physically) is you. They are meant to show you something you are meant to see. Through them, all the gods talk to you. Their language is sensation, feeling and desire.

"Each subpersonality is made up of planetary energies, as you are made of them. They are complexes (thought forms of the archetypes). Each, in their form, has a special message for you (in that they are in *this* form). All together, they show the special meaning of this life to you.

"They are the messengers. You must learn to listen to them all, and understand what they are saying to you and what it signifies. Your relationship is one of "attention to them all"—to listen, to hear, to see, and to know from the inside. To care for, to acknowledge, let be; to educate. They are a family of whom you are the head. The Victim is part of that family. So you must take responsibility for them all. How do you exercise this responsibility? Of what does it consist? You must honor them all—let them be what they are: let them grow. Let them change. Allow them to transform. And allow certain parts of them to die when their creative life is over."

At the next session Joan was ready to resume work with the Victim. This time she said he did not look quite so old or bent, and she did not mind him as much as before. During the session Joan was asked to become the Victim and to really experience his needs; the following conversation ensued.

Therapist: How do you feel?

Victim: Cold very cold.

Therapist: Why?

Victim: Because I am alone, so alone.

Therapist: Why are you alone?

Victim: I am nothing, not important.

Therapist: Tell me why this is so?

Victim: Others come first.

Therapist: Why do they?

Victim: Because I always have to give in to others.

Therapist: How has this happened?

Victim: I am silly.

Therapist: Why?

Victim: I doubt myself.

Therapist: Why do you doubt yourself?

Victim: I always have to give in to others.

Therapist: But why?

Victim: I don't know.

Therapist: Think hard, why do you have to give in to others?

Victim: Because I have no right to anything myself.

Therapist: But why? Who said you had no right to anything yourself?

Victim: I don't know.

Therapist: Think! Where did the idea come from that you had no right to anything, and that you were silly?

Victim: It was my idea.

Therapist: Why did you get such an idea?

Victim: Because I felt resentful. I should not have felt resentful; my mother was busy. It was not her fault. She had no time for me. I felt so guilty about all this resentment; it was wicked of me.

Therapist: Do you believe your mother loved you?

Victim: Yes, that is why I felt so guilty.

Therapist: Do you feel guilty now?

Victim: Not so much.

Therapist: What do you want?

Victim: Attention, love, acceptance.

Therapist: What can you give?

Victim: Nothing.

Therapist: Nothing—have you nothing at all to give?

Victim: I can work, try hard to understand things, learn. I would like that.

Therapist: That would be very good.

At this point in the therapy the Victim is asked to look at Joan and the other subpersonalities, and although feeling shabby and very shy, he joins hands with Joan and the others, experiencing a feeling of belonging and warmth. After Joan had stepped out of the Victim and become Joan again, she turned and looked at the ragged figure. To her surprise, he now seemed much younger and not so dirty and untidy, and she was even beginning to like him.

By refusing to acknowledge the Victim's need for attention, love, and acceptance within her own psyche and with regard to others, she had allowed him to become demanding and deformed. This had brought her pain and loneliness for years because of her refusal to accept his qualities within herself. Joan started working regularly with her subpersonalities, and found the Victim had many positive qualities that she had not been aware of. One was a deep sense of responsibility in her dealings with others, a strong sense of fair play, and sense of duty. Along with these traits was a very persevering nature; all of these qualities were very valuable but needed acknowledgment and acceptance. Joan realized that she had used these qualities in the past, but indiscriminately with no thought for her own needs. In being responsible to others she had given too much. The same thing had happened with her sense of fair play—she had been fair to others but not herself. She began to see that her decisions had to include her own collective needs. Her "duty" was also to her "self."

The persevering part of her nature came in here. She realized she could not change herself overnight. Diligently and quietly she worked on herself, reading all she could to aid her quest. In time she joined a local astrology society, made new friends, and started to entertain at home, realizing that people liked her and enjoyed her company. Instead of feeling negative and blocked, she could now act positively and effectively because of her new-found confidence and strength.

Using a Subpersonality Meditation

Sometimes when you are in a subpersonality looking at "you," this person you see can also be a subpersonality—for instance, you may see yourself as a younger or older person, or different in some way. The house represents our bodies, and special rooms in our houses represent our mind and emotions. The most useful way to work with the subpersonalities is to make a tape of the following meditation.

This Meditation is about a journey. A journey to transform yourself. To become more aware of yourself. It is important to sit comfortably, quietly on your own where you are not likely to be disturbed. Have writing paper by you and a pen or pencil. Take a few minutes to unwind and relax.

Imagine yourself walking along a country lane.
Imagine what the lane is like.
Is it a paved lane?
A stony lane?
What is its surface?
How wide is it?
Are there hedges on either side of you?
What is the countryside like?
What color is the sky?
What time of year is it?
Notice all you can about this lane.
Perhaps it's a lane you know.
There is no need to write anything down now.
Just be in your imagination.
Really imagine yourself there.

Start walking up the lane,
until you come to a dwelling place.
It may be a cottage, a house or bungalow,
or any other type of residence.
When you reach it, just stand outside
and notice what it is built of.
Stone, brick, or other material.
It may have vines growing up it.
Is it large or small?
What is the roof made of?
Tiled, thatch, or another type of material?
Stand outside the front door.
Notice what the front door is like.
Is there a door-knocker?
What color is the door?
If you push the front door it will open.
As it opens, step into the hallway.
In the hallway you will see some doors.
There will be one special door.
You will notice it is closed.
Knock on this door and ask
that someone will come out and speak to you.
Take plenty of time to do this.
There are personalities here
that are very important to you.
One of them will open the door
and come out into the hall.
They may be male or female.
Occasionally an animal will appear.
Take the first personality you see.
And go outside with this personality into the garden.
When outside, stand there and look at this person.
Observe all you can.
Notice how this person stands.
How does this person hold his or her arms and hands?
What clothes are worn?

Start with the feet and work up.
Can you see the face, the hair.
Does he or she wear anything on the head?
Is this person tall, short, or average?
Overweight or slim?
Notice all you can.
Ask this person, "What do you want from me?
What do you need from me? And what have you to offer me?"
Then wait until you hear an answer.
Notice what the answers are,
and, however strange, remember them.
Ask them what they like doing.
Ask them what they do not like doing.
Note the reply.
Then step out of your own body
and into the body of the person
you see standing there.
Fit into this body,
and look out of the eyes at yourself.
Stand like this person stands,
hold your arms and hands
as you saw this person holding his or hers.
Just *feel* what it's like to be this personality.
After you do all this, turn and look at yourself.
How do you see yourself? How old do you look?
How do you feel being this personality—looking at you?
Do you like what you see?
What do you feel?
Tell the person that used to be you what you want.
When you have experienced as much as
you want to experience today,
step back into you again.
When you have done this,
turn and look at the personality again.
Do you feel differently about them now,
or do you still feel the same?

What are your feelings to this personality?
Do you like it?
Has the personality changed in any way?
If there is anything special you want to say
to this personality, say it.
Is there anything you think you can do to help this personality?
If so, do it.

Say goodbye to this person you met for now
and walk back into the house.
Write down any notes.
Repeat the same exercise to meet another subpersonality.

At the end of the meeting with the second,
third, fourth, or even fifth subpersonality
let all the subpersonalities meet.
Notice how they do or do not get on together.

Go back and work with them as many times as necessary.
Identify them in your actions.
Recognize at certain times during the day
which one is in charge.
Which ones do not get on together?
What can you do to enable them
to have a more harmonious relationship?

It is important to keep notes
on all your experiences,
for as in dreams, they can be quickly lost.

Part III

PLUTO

Esculapiuus, Serapis, Pluto, Knoun and Kneph are all the deities with the attributes of the serpent. Says Dupuis, "They are all healers, givers of health, spiritual and physical, and of enlightenment."

—————*Madame Blavatsky*

Pluto in Mythology, Literature, and Art

If Saturn has long been regarded as the disciplinarian of the universe, the mysterious planet, Pluto has been even less favorably received. In the ancient legends, Pluto was one of the three sons of Saturn who rebelled against their father and seized control of the kingdom. They divided it into three parts: Jupiter took Olympus and the heavens, Neptune took the seas, and Pluto became lord of the underworld. Immediately, Pluto became everyone's destiny, the ultimate overlord. As such he was feared, revered, and avoided as long as possible! There were no temples to Pluto, no altars. Myths about him often involve travelers to his kingdom who struggle to return from whence they came. At best the image of Pluto is of dark and mysterious fate; at worst he conjures up visions of sinister shadows and threatening disintegration. He is the lord of death with all its consequent terror and despair.

But perhaps the essential qualities of Pluto can make us believe otherwise. Perhaps there is a more favorable way to look at the myths and the fables of Pluto. The negative qualities of this gloomy kingdom and its helmeted ruler whose face remains shrouded from sight may be counterbalanced by positive elements which tend to be ignored. This denial is unfortunate because ancient myths are a mirror of intuitive truth, and the wisdom behind the stories is to be appreciated as a whole picture, both positive and negative.

The most famous fable about Pluto is his love for Persephone, the daughter of Ceres, the Goddess of Harvest. Pluto was driving his chariot with black horses on the earth, when he was smitten by an arrow from Cupid and promptly fell in love with the girl who was gathering flowers in a wood. He swooped down and carried her off, ignoring her cries and screams. In Hades she became his queen and gradually accepted her fate, appreciating the love and power her husband bestowed on her. Neverthe-less, above ground, Ceres continued to search for her and the harvest was delayed while she hunted high and low for her daughter. Eventually, the spirit of the river that ran into Hades—Alpheus—told her where Perse-phone had been taken and she promptly appealed to Jupiter for help. A compromise was reached: Jupiter would gain the girl's release as long as she had not eaten anything during her stay in the underworld. But cunning Pluto had fed her a pomegranate and Persephone was lost; he cared enough for her, however, to release her for six months of the year on the condition that she returned to him for the rest of the time. Ceres was pacified, and during her daughter's earth visits, she restored springtime and harvest to mankind. When Persephone went back to her husband, the earth "died" again.

The parable here is quite obvious: the fertility cycle demands a period of darkness and death in order to be reborn. The flowers and the pomegran-ate both represent the seeds of life, and the actual rape of Persephone by Pluto is a sexual act, although the ancients were careful to stress the love, respect, power, and dignity that were bestowed on her afterwards. For Persephone, the suffering brought fulfillment to herself and the earth; the price was high but there was no other way of releasing her potential. In this way, "life" and "death" are seen to be two sides of the same coin and symbiotic.

In the *Aeneid*, Virgil's hero Aeneas, the Trojan warrior, is taken into the underworld by Anchises. There he is shown the souls grouped in Pluto's kingdom—and he is amazed to see both his ancestors *and* his descendants. He is told: "These are souls whose destiny it is to live a second time in this body."[1] In other words, the realm of Pluto is concerned with the future as well as the past. It is a world of mystery rather than fear, of enigma rather than obliteration. From these depths spring energies of renewal, strength, and enlightenment. "Pluto" comes from *pluton,* a Latin word meaning "riches," and the Romans saw him as a god of wealth.

But he is also obscure, and to find him necessitates pain, resilience, and determination. None of the travelers to his kingdom have an easy time. Ceres experienced despair and exhaustion in her quest. So did Orpheus,

---

[1] Virgil, *Aeneid*, Book VI, lines 688-720, translated by W. F. Jackson Knight (London: Penguin, 1956), p. 168.

who, in another story, descended into Hades to find his lost love, Eurydice. He moved Persephone and Pluto with the strength of his love and the power of his music, and he was granted his wife's return to the earth on the condition that he did not look back at her on their journey out of the underworld. In his impatience to see her again, he forgot the promise and turned back to her, and so lost her forever.

Again we see a vision of Pluto that is neither negative nor uncompromising. The ruler of the ultimate mystery is sensitive and encouraging. He is prepared to meet the aspiring soul halfway. His conditions are strenuous but also attainable: the price is never so high that it cannot be paid with discipline, determination, and single-mindedness. The passion and pain involved are essentially transitional.

For several writers and poets, the myth of Pluto has become symbolic of all artistic creation. The fertility of the imagination is a mirror of the fertility of the earth, and the painful cost of bearing fruit is reflected in the struggle of Ceres.

> . . . *Prosérpine gathering flowers*
> *Herself a fairer flower, by gloomy Dis*
> *Was gathered—which cost Ceres all that pain*
> *To seek her through the world.*[2]

Orpheus was the supreme musician, yet he had to descend into the bowels of the earth to seek his soul. Love and art have long been equated (in many cultures, making love is regarded as an art form), but the formidable challenge of the quest for love—or art—or the soul cannot be denied. In this quest, Pluto is seen as a figure of risk and challenge, often associated with violation and intrusion. He raped his wife, he demands his price. He rewards but also dictates. He is the secret part of the personality, the very depths of which are occasionally glimpsed, and realized in artistic creation, or spiritual searching, or sexual fulfillment.

Coleridge illustrated this perfectly with his poem "Kubla Khan"—a fragment supposedly written after a deep three-hour sleep. It deals with the act of artistic creation and describes a glorious pleasure dome and gardens

---

[2] John Milton, *Paradise Lost,* Book IV, lines 269-272, from *Poems and Selected Prose,* edited by Hope Nicholson (New York: Bantam Classic, 1962), p. 278.

built over caves of ice and a chasm that leads down to a "sunless sea." It is significant that the river that descends through the caverns is none other than the River Alph (Alpheus)—the same river that spoke to Ceres and told her the truth about her daughter. In the poem, the "savage, holy and enchanted place" is haunted by love songs and "seething" fountains and "dancing" rocks. Its passage into the depths of the earth is one of violence and "ceaseless turmoil." Yet the poet is left with stunning impressions of Paradise: heavenly music, the miracle of the floating dome, and the sensation of ecstasy. The whole experience is seen as a mystical ritual.

> *Weave a circle round him thrice,*
> *And close your eyes with holy dread,*
> *For he on honey-dew hath fed*
> *And drunk the milk of paradise.*[3]

In the 20th century, T. S. Eliot endorses the same identification of creative potential: his "Four Quartets" explore the passage of the seasons with the passage of the soul, and the quest for fulfillment. In "The Waste Land," he could envisage no fulfillment—just a waiting for rain in a parched desert landscape (cf., "Saturn in Mythology, Literature, and Art, pp. 13-16). But in "East Coker," he takes the quest a stage further, daring to speculate on the hidden harmony that is the destiny of all. Again, his souls dance in mystic circles, creating a ritualistic power that magnifies their oneness with time and with the seasons.

> *In that open field*
> *If you do not come too close, if you do not come too close*
> *On a summer midnight, you can hear the music. . .*
> *And see them dancing around the bonfire*
> *The association of man and woman*
> *In daunsinge, signifying matrimonie—*
> *Two and Two, necessarye coniunction,. . .*
> *Whiche betokeneth concorde. . .*

---

[3] Samuel Taylor Coleridge, "Kubla Khan," edited by Earnest Hartley Coleridge (Oxford: Oxford University Press, 1969), lines 51-54.

> *Earth Feet, loam feet, lifted in country mirth*
> *Mirth of those long since under earth*
> *Nourishing the corn. Keeping time. . .*[4]

Here the fertility dance is taking place over the dead, and the magic circle of "concorde" is the product of love *and* lust: the natural rhythm of life. In this respect, lust is seen as both necessary and desirable—a means of restoring "nourishment"—and descent into the darkness is inevitable in order to achieve *oneness* with the elements in an orgasmic disintegration.

> *The houses are all gone under the sea.*
> *The dancers are all gone under the hill.*[5]

Eliot goes on to describe this darkness as "the darkness of God," and charts the descent into chaos as traveling on an underground train with no light between stations and only the unreal feeling of terror and suspense. But then his darkness becomes a creative darkness—the darkness becomes light, the stillness becomes dancing, and he hears the music of running water. Like Coleridge, he sees himself in a garden of paradise.

> *The laughter in the garden, echoed ecstasy*
> *Not lost, but requiring, pointing to the agony*
> *Of death and birth.*[6]

This is the Pluto experience—the agony of death in order to realize birth, the struggle to search deep inside the subconscious to achieve harmony and creativity and fullest consciousness. This is the message of the ancients in their portrayal of Pluto as the Lord of Darkness: he is the destiny of all through the individual's dissolution, symbolic death, sexuality and transcendence. He cannot be avoided—but he mirrors the brightest as well as the darkest self inside each of us.

---

[4] T. S. Eliot, "East Coker," lines 24-39.
[5] T. S. Eliot, "East Coker," lines 99-100.
[6] T. S. Eliot, "East Coker," lines 131-133.

Here and there does not matter
We must be still and still moving
Into another intensity
For a further union, a deeper communion. . .
In my end is my beginning.[7]

---

[7] T. S. Eliot, "East Coker," lines 203-209.

How to Understand Pluto by Sign and House

Pluto will stay in the same sign for several years, affecting whole generations with its influence. From 1912/13/14 until 1937/38/39, Pluto was in the sign of Cancer.[8] The generation born with Pluto in Cancer suffered greatly as two world wars broke up homes and families, causing tremendous emotional suffering. Pluto's placement in the fourth house shows in a generic way how this influence may affect a whole generation. During the years that Pluto went permanently into Cancer (1914) and Leo (1939) respectively, the First and Second World Wars started.

Pluto in Leo (1937/38/39—1956/57/58) brought in the I AM IMPORTANT generation. This generation carried an inner need for each individual to be unique and creative in his or her own right, and it was concerned with developing everything connected to individual enjoyment and fulfillment. Pluto in Leo is similar, although in a very general way, to Pluto in the fifth house.

The Pluto in Virgo generation (1956/57/58—1971/72) is at this present time experiencing mass unemployment and great changes in work and economy, particularly within the West, as well as mass starvation throughout the World (Virgo is also connected to food and diet). Many power struggles revolve around work and service within this group. Pluto in the sixth house will show, in a very generalized way, how this influence may be experienced by a generation.

The Pluto in Libra generation (1971/72—1983/84) is still very young, and their adult group experience is still almost unknown. Pluto in Libra is similar to Pluto in the seventh house. The oldest among this group—now approaching their 20s—are already witnessing great power

---

[8] Please see the Pluto table, Appendix II, page 184, for the exact dates.

struggles between world leaders, where those with the greatest weapons call the tune, where underhanded dealings and manipulation seem the norm. Each generation will experience life through its own Pluto placement, as well as going through the transmutation connected to the following generations and their Pluto placements.

We have only to wonder what the Pluto in Scorpio children will inherit and experience, as Pluto moves into the fixed constellations beyond Scorpio. Pluto in the eighth house provides a loose interpretation of Pluto in Scorpio.

Pluto is the outer planet of our solar system and takes 248.5 years to orbit the Sun. Pluto can spend as long as thirty years or more in each sign. Pluto will stay only twelve years in the sign of Scorpio, however, due to the law of relativity.[9] For a proportion of Pluto's 248 year orbit, the planet is actually closer to the Sun than Neptune. At the present time, Pluto's elliptical orbit is within the orbit of Neptune. This will be so from 1979 to 1999.

Pluto brings into this life a residue of obsessions and impulses that often carry over from past existences. In order for anyone to be able to let go of the past, Pluto's influence needs to be investigated and worked with. In working with this god, old needs to dominate and control are transmuted into a higher awareness of the unity of all life. No longer are power struggles so important, or the ability for applause or respect or any other false and personal needs we may hold. Pluto's power for transformation is great but only when the energy is used in an impersonal way.

Pluto can help to destroy old structures that are no longer viable within the current life. This is necessary before his wealth—which is often considerable—can be unearthed or reborn. However, while purely personal considerations motivate the personality, no rebirth is possible. It is sometimes after periods of intense personal crisis that the person concerned can learn to let go of the past and many of the negative impulses attached to it. This time often, although not always, coincides with a person's mid-life crisis—when Pluto squares Pluto, triggering off any aspects connected to this planet. Pluto's transits are always centered around the process of death and rebirth of the personality.

---

[9] When a planet's orbit is at its nearest point to the Sun, an increased acceleration takes place.

Because Pluto will stay in the same sign for several years, the house that Pluto occupies in each individual chart will show the more personalized way that Pluto's influence will make itself felt within the individual personality. Aspects to Pluto on the natal chart should also be seen as very important, particularly those aspects to the Sun, Moon, or Ascendant. When reading the following, take note of the house Pluto rules, or co-rules, as this also has significance, although it is obviously a more minor one.

PLUTO IN ARIES (OR THE 1ST HOUSE)

Pluto in the first house denotes that any power struggles in life may be aimed at guarding your own self-identity. Often you will experience difficulties through relationships, for others are sometimes seen as a threat. Cooperation with others is necessary with this position of Pluto. At the same time, any relationship, particularly those on a deep personal level, is very difficult for you to maintain, due to the unconscious tendency to protect and control your own personal concerns—sometimes at the expense of other people's considerations and needs.

There is a great and unconscious need within you to protect yourself and your own self-interests. You may deeply distrust life, feeling that others are out to get you. Because of this, you may sometimes display a certain degree of unscrupulous action in self-guarding yourself and getting what you want.

Occasionally Pluto in the first house can give some physical or mental disability, and therefore, the struggle in life can be aimed at overcoming this difficulty, as well as others' prejudices.

To investigate this position, you must understand Saturn's message as well as Pluto's. Once the former is truly understood, great inner transformation can begin. Until then, you will be no more than a slave to Pluto's very strong unconscious and controlling influence, which will cause you to be drawn into all sorts of power games throughout your life, some of which may be quite unpleasant.

While you maintain certain attitudes that are basically aimed at getting your own way, Pluto will control you unmercifully, and it may help you to realize that any position of Pluto is only difficult while it remains unconscious. As soon as you begin to understand Saturn and Pluto's influence in your life, wonderful shifts in consciousness start to occur, and power games with others will no longer be so important.

Difficult aspects to Pluto in the first house will intensify any negative reactions, while positive aspects will give the ability for great transformation within your personal identity and the path towards selfhood. This position of Pluto can also signify someone who has considerable power to heal others as well as themselves.[10]

PLUTO IN TAURUS (OR THE 2ND HOUSE)

The second house is concerned with our inner values and resources, as well as the money we earn and our possessions. Pluto in this house will show that transformation is needed in some if not all of these areas.

Within your life you will struggle to hang on to your own values and beliefs. Often there will be power struggles around what you believe and want out of life. Others will be expected to give in to you and follow your requirements. With this position of Pluto, there is some inbuilt stubbornness that stops any transformation taking place. Rigidity is common, and fixed opinions are a stumbling block.

Money and possessions in some form are a big issue in your life; usually you will have a high earning power, and compulsive habits often keep you tied to the wheel in order to prove your values and capabilities to others.

It is when you start to recognize the need for higher values within your world that transformation starts to take place, but until this happens, and while you put material concerns and society's values forever in the forefront of your mind, you are again stuck in old patterns of unproductive behavior.

If you start to recognize your need to see others, as well as the world in general, fit into your own belief system, you can start to shed some of your self-created chains, but until this happens you will disagree with

---

[10] I have observed this aspect in the charts of powerful healers, particularly when Pluto conjuncts the ascendant, but have also noticed that sometimes when the persons concerned were not able to detach from Pluto's more negative manifestations, they tended to be used by the energy rather than consciously working with it. In some cases, this manifested as rather megalomaniacal tendencies.

everyone who does not share your plans, opinions, or ideals. Insight into your own real need for transformation may be lost. Investigate Saturn's position to see why you have a need to hang on to outworn values that have little place or meaning in your life. Positive aspects to Pluto will help you to begin to recognize and to shed old and outdated value systems. More difficult aspects to Pluto may slow up this process, blocking recognition of where conversion is needed within your life.

PLUTO IN GEMINI (OR THE 3RD HOUSE)

With Pluto in the third house, it is likely your mind will be very deep and penetrating, the speech often sharp and to the point, usually aimed at making the best of every opportunity. Words are often used very carefully and with great deliberation—although in certain situations, speech may be guarded in order to protect your own interests.

This position of Pluto bestows a deep and penetrating mind, and a certain type of mental manipulation over others is often observed. You are the sort of person who wants your own way and will often go to great lengths to achieve this. You are out to win and do not always mind how you go about it. Self-doubt to you is akin to death, but sometimes during your life, it may be necessary in order for you to bring about greater understanding.

You may sometimes push your own ideas onto others, perhaps feeling you are right and others are wrong. Because of the force you put into your speech, others may reject their own thoughts in favor of what you believe. When you realize the power of your words, also accepting that your belief system may not always be right, transformation can begin. But while you hang on to your own ideas with little regard for others, you will end up reaping that which you have sown. The universe works in perfect harmony, and certain ideas perpetrated by you will eventually come home to roost. Whether these ideas are productive or destructive will depend on your own personal point of view at the time.

The more you can understand your own human drives and motivation, the more your words and thoughts can be used to help and transform, not just your own life but also the lives of others. However, this can only happen after your thoughts become more impersonally oriented—after you have fully investigated and understood Saturn's as well as Pluto's deeper messages. Otherwise you are forever giving others advice based on your own inner pain. Difficult aspects to Pluto may block the acceptance of a more impersonal thought pattern. Positive aspects to Pluto will help the mind to shed old ideas and thought patterns, and give the ability to heal many ills, both in the world and as within your own mind.

PLUTO IN CANCER (OR THE 4TH HOUSE)

Pluto in the fourth house shows that transformation in this lifetime will come about through understanding your deepest emotional needs. This is not always easy for you, as you learned much of this unconscious information when very young.

It is likely that power struggles developed at an early age within the family; one or more parents may have been controlling, never allowing spontaneous reactions. This control on the level of your emotive needs then becomes a normal reaction within you. You may either control your emotional responses in order to get your own way or use emotional power games to make others beholden to you. At times you can overpower those you care for. There may be a type of smother love connected to your giving, but normally when you give this type of love you want a great deal in return, and when others realize this, they may back away, leaving you bitterly disappointed when you do not get back from others what you so earnestly desire.

Emotionally, you may still want to be a child with no real emotional responsibility connected to giving and receiving within your relationships. If you look carefully, you may see that many of your emotional needs and desires stem from this impulse. Emotionally, therefore, you need to grow up and base your emotional responses on reality, not on what you experienced as a very young child; for until you do this, possessiveness, jealousy, anger, and fear are the unconscious forces that will control your life.

It is likely that you will find it difficult to get away from the family influence, particularly your mother's effect on you. You may even find yourself trapped in some way within the family situation. However, should this happen, you should investigate the reason why—for example, is going back to mother or the family the only way you can really feel needed?

Try and investigate the fears and phobias that stem from your childhood. To do this, understand fully Saturn's as well as Pluto's position. If you do this honestly, you may start to free yourself from past conditioning. If you refuse, you will find that life will continually pull the rug out from under your feet, forcing you to reject the old patterns of childhood, and to accept new and more productive patterns of emotional behavior.

Try and realize you can reach a new level of emotional understanding, but this will only come about when you begin to master your feelings through understanding your deepest dreads and fears. Difficult aspects to Pluto in the fourth will block the shedding of old emotional patterns, and so each difficult aspect should be studied and understood in order for you to be able to start to "let go." Positive aspects to Pluto in the fourth will facilitate an easier shedding of old emotional habits and needs.

PLUTO IN LEO (OR THE 5TH HOUSE)

The fifth house is the house of the Self, children, creative expression, as well as the house of love affairs, enjoyment, and pleasure. With Pluto in the fifth house transformation usually centers around these issues.

Pride and arrogance are often the unconscious motivation for many of your actions, as well as the need to establish yourself and somehow be seen as a person of importance. These considerations can lead you to a great deal of compulsive behavior, and your more creative talents may be lost as a result.

Your love affairs will frequently exhibit great intensity, and there may be some vanity involved with issues that center around your affections. You will want to be seen as a person of some importance within any emotional involvement, and self-respect, not to say at times conceit, will play an important role in any deep and meaningful involvement. Within your love affairs and emotional entanglements, you may want to dominate and control. If this is the case, look to your Saturn placement as well as investigating Pluto's role. This will help you to more fully understand why you need so much power and domination in these areas. Children, both as your creations and as your emotional offspring, can also teach you many things about yourself.

There is a wealth of creativity to be tapped within this placement of Pluto, but first negative and destructive tendencies should be investigated. The enormous need for acclaim and approval should be looked at realistically, for fears connected to these issues may well block any more creative tendencies from ever manifesting. Your need to be the greatest and best at whatever you do may well cause your abilities to be continually thwarted. For this reason, you should thoroughly transform your tendencies to "do" within the world in to tendencies to "be." When this transformation occurs, the influence from Pluto's motivation can be strong enough to bring out the greatest creative ability within you at a most brilliant power and depth. Positive aspects to Pluto will facilitate this creativity being brought into existence and fruition. Negative aspects will keep you tied to past dependencies that revolve around personal recognition for yourself based on pride, arrogance, and vanity.

PLUTO IN VIRGO (OR THE 6TH HOUSE)

The sixth house deals with work, service, health, and diet, as well as those we may employ. Pluto seeks transformation on some if not all of these levels.

You will have a strong urge at times to be of use to others. This may be through your work or in some other area of service. If this is not achieved in full, you will at least want to feel you are a help in some way. This help also includes that support and assistance that you give to family, friends, or colleagues. However, Pluto's obsessional tendencies can at times cause you to take on too much work—whatever that work entails—and painful episodes can ensue when other people feel threatened by your indomitable will, which will direct many of your actions in this area.

Sometimes this position of Pluto causes you to thoroughly overwork yourself to the point of a breakdown. You may work compulsively and yet, at the same time, really resent having to do so. Always in the work situation, the need to come out on top seems necessary to you. When this is not achieved power struggles with co-workers or associates can ensue. Look to Saturn's position within your chart to see why you have a constant need to prove yourself. It may even be better for you if you work alone; for in that way, you work for yourself, and unnecessary domination and/or power struggles within the work front are thus avoided.

Although work, as well as service to others, is a necessary part of your life, you may at times severely resent what this entails. You may be put upon by family and friends, as well as by bosses and coworkers. When this happens, you should investigate further just why this has occurred. Often it will be because you give out unconscious signals that you can take on anything and still come out on top. This may be the result of your total need for power and control on the work front, and when recognized for such, it can be channelled into wonderful fruitfulness and fertility—both materially and spiritually. But this only happens when you become less personally concerned with all you do for others, as well as with all you achieve in the area of labor and craftsmanship.

Positive aspects to Pluto will enable you to move forward and drop any compulsive needs. Difficult aspects will tie you to the past where obsessive forces keep your nose to the grindstone and your hand to the wheel, despite any resentments and unwillingness on your part.

Sometimes health may be the vehicle through which Pluto focuses, and any severe health breakdown may be a warning that there are deep psychological problems that need investigating. Sometimes ill health is used to manipulate and control others, although this is usually an unconscious impulse and is not brought about through any conscious intention.

PLUTO IN LIBRA (OR THE 7TH HOUSE)

Pluto in the seventh house suggests that power struggles will center around the need for domination within your deepest relationships. The partner you choose will often be of a Plutonian type, and a great deal of your own negativity will be projected onto him or her. Power struggles will be rife as each of you battles to win domination over the other. Sometimes this domination is very subtle, and you may often refuse to accept your own part in what is actually happening.

It is only when you can start to accept your own shadow side, which you see mirrored in your partner—as well as in other people—that transformation will start to commence. To begin accepting your own shadow might be very difficult initially, but until you accept some part in the battles that are taking place, the same pattern will repeat itself again and again.

When you begin to realize that power can be positive just as well as negative, you may be able to start re-claiming some of this Plutonic energy. Look at what you actually experience from your partner as well as other people—all the negatives such as greed, anger, jealousy, and manipulation. Try to stop blaming them for everything that you see happening, and try to accept some of the responsibility yourself. Also, look carefully and at length at what your real needs are in your relationship. To do this, first investigate Saturn's position and aspects within the chart, then look at Pluto's.

You may find that some of your difficulties with others may arise because of how you think others perceive you. These ideas you need to transform. You desperately may want to express and show others your real nature and identity, but somehow this is very difficult for you to do, and hostility will constantly surface.

Once you stop battling with others, you will start to see your place in life more clearly, and wonderful transformations can start to happen—but this is only after you accept some of your shadow side. Positive aspects to Pluto will help you to let go of past habits within relationships; negative aspects will cause unconscious blocks within your psyche, causing you to refuse to accept any part in what is happening.

PLUTO IN SCORPIO (OR THE 8TH HOUSE)

Pluto is the ruler of the eighth house and so is in its natural place here. The eighth house is connected to sex, death, as well as in-depth psychology. It is also connected to our shared resources with others, such as those that exist within deep sexual and emotional entanglements. The eighth house also involves others' money as well as others' values and resources, and thus, it can also be associated with tax and inheritance. Pluto's influence here may center around many issues connected to giving and receiving in the broadest sense. Therefore, with Pluto in the eighth house, you will go through deep and transforming experiences connected to many of the above issues—although some of them will certainly be very deep, obscure, and exceptionally hard to recognize.

Pluto in the eighth house will force you to face many obsessive impulses in the areas of mutual sharing with others. Sexual and emotional encounters may be full of deep and hidden compulsions, but ultimately can be an area of great learning and transformation. In these encounters, you will often have to face great emotional pain, and at times, you may even feel that something has died within you. Always remember when you feel like this that something within you has to die in order for something much more precious to be reborn. Much of your learning will center around your need to be in control on both an emotional and sexual level. Much of this control will go on within yourself making spontaneity extremely difficult. To understand why you have the need for such controls, look to Saturn's position on your chart, as well as investigating Pluto's deeper implications.

On a material level Pluto in the eighth house can signify business partnerships, or any form of agreement in which money and resources play a part. Its position in the eighth house helps you understand your own deepest reasons for forming, as well as needing, the association in the first place.

Pluto in the eighth house gives you tremendous power for transformation, as well as releasing some of your own hidden talents. This happens at the time in your life when you realize your disappointment for much of the material world, and so learn to devote more time to your real needs. At times, difficult aspects to Pluto will block your need to let go of past emotional, sexual, and material dependencies. Positive aspects will enable you to let go, to move on, and to never look back.

PLUTO IN SAGITTARIUS (OR THE 9TH HOUSE)

The ninth house represents higher wisdom and understanding, one's relationship with god, the law, legal matters, morality, learning beyond high school, philosophy, as well as foreign travel and long journeys—both of the mind, body, and imagination. The ninth house is concerned with our search for meaning in life and is the house associated with thoughts that are beyond the limits of purely human consciousness. Pluto in this position can cause unconscious blocks and controls that can stop the expression of the Higher Mind from manifesting. As the ninth house experience covers many areas, there are a great many ways in which Pluto in the ninth house may be expressed.

With Pluto in the ninth house, knowledge and understanding may be used as power over oneself or over others, in various and diverse ways.

Dane Rudhyar believes that "the danger one faces in terms of ninth house experience is overexpansion caused by ambition and greed for power or the symbol of social power, money." He goes on to say that "ambition is the negative aspect of understanding, for it implies a compulsive egocentric approach to human relationships."[11] Pluto in this house can add to this overexpansion and need for power.

With Pluto in the ninth house religion, god, and a higher philosophy in life are often seen as powerful forces that can take away personal freedom. The unconscious control going on here can manifest through others, and their religious views, which are usually strongly resisted. This position can make you so adamant in regard to your own deliberations that others rarely have a bearing on any of your own philosophical views. You may even attempt to control others with your own pet concepts and theories. You may strongly resist the need to attend college, or university, or, in fact, resist any attempt from others who—for whatever reason—desire you to learn.

It may happen that sometime in your life, you do meet someone who profoundly transforms your views on god and the universe. Another manifestation of this position is that your life may be greatly changed by someone from another culture or race. However, the above changes are usually accompanied by power struggles and/or traumatic events that shake the very foundations of your soul.

Morality can be another area of difficulty for you. You may feel completely controlled by moral obligations, and/or have a desire to break through all moral codes, regardless of others' rights or justifications. Breaking the law, whether on the material or spiritual levels, often occurs because of this inner desire to beat whatever it is stopping you from doing what you want. You may try to beat society's moral code or even your own inner ethics. Legal battles and power struggles may also ensue.

Freedom in itself is certainly very important to you, and often, you will feel that other people—even life itself—are somehow threatening to take this very freedom from you. When you realize that the jailer is inside yourself and that in order to be free, you must explore your inner being, then great changes take place. Look also to Saturn's position on your chart to begin understanding what it is you can learn about restriction and how it can eventually lead to true freedom.

---

[11] Dane Rudhyar, *The Astrological Houses* (Sebastopol, CA: CRCS Publications, 1986), p. 115.

Positive aspects to Pluto help you see beyond your prison, to all the possibilities that exist once you face your own inner self. Hard aspects to Pluto seem to stop you taking the next step in self-discovery and keep you going over many of the old paths that lead away from Self and from the path of self-transformation.

PLUTO IN CAPRICORN (OR THE 10TH HOUSE)

The tenth house is associated with the world, career, and all authority figures, including your parents. It is in the tenth house where you will experience failure or success when trying to gain a social, public, or professional place within the medium of the world, as well as within your own environment. The tenth house is also the house of achievement.

With Pluto in the tenth house, you may have the urge to succeed in a career or in having a place of power within the world—even employing ruthless means at times to achieve your ends—or you may suffer power struggles through your career or through your need to succeed in the world. Another manifestation of Pluto in the tenth house is having to experience manipulative games, particularly from those with authority over you.

Pluto in the tenth house can also give you quite a fear of the world. The world can seem a threatening place, and you either spend a great deal of time trying to come to terms with this dilemma or you try and beat the world at all costs.

When you were younger, one parent may have been particularly manipulative and controlling. This can manifest as a deep resentment to anyone in power or authority. This obviously can cause many problems as you continually battle against the very success and acceptance you seek within the world order. Saturn is the natural ruler of the tenth house, so in trying to understand Pluto's message, also remember to look to Saturn's position in your chart for a clearer understanding on the above matters—particularly those connected to authority figures. It may be that because of your deep distrust of authority in all forms, counseling or psychotherapy may be difficult. Therefore, working on an inner level with Saturn as well as with Pluto may be particularly beneficial to you.

Positive aspects to Pluto will help you transform your own ego's need for power into a universal acceptance of power used only for the good of the society you live in. Difficult aspects will keep you tied longer to your unconscious need for power, which is based on fear connected to the world and the environment you live in.

PLUTO IN AQUARIUS (OR THE 11TH HOUSE)

The eleventh house is the house of friends, groups, and associations, including your peer group. The eleventh house is also the house connected with your dreams, hopes, and aspirations. Pluto in this house will bring powerful forces of transformation into either one or more of these areas.

Friends, groups, and organizations can often play a large part within your life, although within this order, control games are often experienced. The control can sometimes be quite insidious, and therefore, it may take time for you to recognize exactly what is going on in certain situations. Likewise, you may feel the need for control within the group, but if you can work towards transforming your own inner powers, you can begin to manifest leadership qualities of the greatest value. However, should your need for power within the group outweigh your own need for transformation, many battles for predominance may be the outcome, with much bitterness and recrimination. Look to Saturn's position on your chart for more insight into why you have such difficulties in the above areas.

You may choose friends who try to manipulate or control you or those that behave in an underhand and devious way towards you. When you recognize exactly what is happening with certain friends or acquaintances, it is inevitable that they either fade out, pass away, or are transformed into something more in keeping with your own true needs for comradeship and brotherhood.

There may be one or more friendships of the greatest importance during this lifetime, friendships that endure over many years, even through long separations. It is through real and lasting comradeship that great transformation can take place as you give up many of your old ego needs to support someone you know, like, and trust.

The eleventh house also is the house associated with hopes, dreams, and aspirations, and so these, too, can either be a source for transformation and/or control within your unconscious mind. Your hopes and dreams may be the controlling factor within your life, which may cause you to disassociate from life rather than take part in it. This can cause loneliness and isolation. However, there may be certain periods during your life when you choose to go into solitude. These can be transforming periods if they become a prerequisite in your search for Self.

Positive aspects to Pluto show the areas of growth and transformation in the above areas. Difficult aspects show where old behavior patterns are unconsciously sabotaging your own need to let go of the old ways of being, stopping you from being reborn on a higher level of cognition within the group experience.

PLUTO IN PISCES (OR THE 12TH HOUSE)

The twelfth house represents your unconscious mind, confinement, and sacrifice, as well as karma from previous lives. With Pluto in this house, you may be drawn into situations with others in which you often end up being the victim. It seems important, therefore, that you begin to realize—if this is the case—that you yourself may be unconsciously using your Plutonic energy to get back at others. Instead of blaming other people, you may need to understand what power being the "victim" gives you. Certainly in close relationships you can make others feel guilty over how they react to you, but if you begin to realize your own part in what is taking place, you can go through a tremendous transformation, as you let go of old and outworn patterns of behavior that are no longer relevant to your current life.

You may begin to recognize that many of the unpleasant situations you experience with others have no bearing on what is actually going on now and are only unconscious memories from a dim and distant past. Something deep within you seems to sabotage many of the things that are important to you. Another way you may use this energy is to sacrifice yourself for others, but this "sacrifice" usually has quite a few strings and conditions attached if you look carefully.

As the twelfth house can be the most difficult of all the houses to understand, time should be taken to analyze and meditate on what is really going on within your interrelations with others, especially those where you are duped or appear to become the butt for others' shortcomings, receiving criticism, blame, and even persecution at times.

You may spend long periods alone, or in the midst of great activity, you may feel lonely and unwanted. The isolation is sometimes necessary for you to gain strength and can lead to great inner understanding taking place. This position does give you the ability to let go of past pains and hurts, as well as all the fears and obsessions that go with them. In order to put this process to work, start to recognize Saturn's and Pluto's position in your chart, as well as the aspects connected to both planets, then use this information to let go of the past and to move on to a more productive pattern in the future.

This position can bestow great spirituality, but it can only manifest when you let go of past needs and desires that no longer have any place in this lifetime. Often your unconscious demands will center around your ego's own requirements for having some importance, as well as recognition and gratitude in connection to all your giving and sacrificing.

Positive aspects to Pluto will expedite this transformation, while difficult aspects will cause past needs and grievances to keep you locked into old behavior patterns that have no further place in your current life.

Working with the Pluto Meditation

In astrology, Pluto is the ruler of all hidden things, including karma, occult knowledge, depth psychology, magic, sex and the procreative urge, healing, kundalini, transformation, and death. Also, it is the energy that fuels all those hidden, primordial drives and desires of our human nature, the natural urge to survive. The planet Pluto was discovered in 1930 around the same time we discovered Plutonium. This volcanic atomic energy is symbolic of the force that Pluto contains. Its destructive force is not to be taken lightly, nor can it always be safely contained. Power-hungry people and large organizations wielding power over others are also symbolic of Pluto. The energy of Pluto can shift mountains, can destroy and abuse; it is also the survival force in nature, the dominance of the fittest, ruthless control and repression. But it can also heal, regenerate, create, transform, and transcend.

Most of us—including those who seek some form of answer to life and those on a spiritual path, whatever that may be—suffer both sides of Pluto's generosity. We can be aware of energies that truly do enable us to achieve better spiritual or mental health or awareness, and, at the same time, we can suffer from dominating and obsessive impulses over which we appear to have no control. The same criteria applies to all manner of people using power over others: they are often being used by the very energy they themselves appear to be using.

Pluto and Saturn are both lords of karma. Saturn is the disciplinarian, the god who, through what appears to be great limitations and hardship, eventually brings us to the realization that until we take responsibility for ourselves and our actions, we will continually create more difficulties to work through. Pluto is the god who stores and releases karma for us—to help us, willingly or unwillingly, to bring hidden desires to the surface to be dealt with, and to redeem those aspects of our natures—the creative and positive factions—that dwell within.

PLUTO AND PLANETARY ENERGY

Pluto is a planet of impersonal energy, of transcendence; so what happens when we use the energy from this planet for our own personal benefits? The myth of Orpheus needs to be understood here: Orpheus was told not to look back for to look back was symbolically to succumb to his own personal desire—and by doing this, he lost what he so dearly loved, Eurydice. Eliphas Levi in *The Key to the Mysteries* describes it so.

> But, woe to the lover if he changes the magnetic current and pursues in his turn with a single look, her whom he should only attract! The sacred love, the virginal love, the love which is stronger than the tomb, seeks only devotion, and flies in terror before the egoism of desire. Orpheus knows it; but, for an instant, he forgets it. [12]

In forgetting, Orpheus loses his love which is dearer to him than all else, and is thus destined to wander alone for the rest of his life. There is no denying the Pluto energy: we have to experience it, but on what level and how? There is, as Eliphas Levi suggests, a two-way magnetic current from Pluto. This brings to mind Medusa, the hydra-haired gorgon whose looks turned people to stone. Dante in his vision of hell descends with an angel to the city of Dis, where he discovers that heretics are punished in tombs burning with intense fire in this city of grief. He passes on with Virgil and eventually comes to the place of the female furies and Medusa and is told:

> *E'en when by Theseus' might assailed, we took*
> *No ill revenge. "Turn thyself round, and keep*
> *Thy countenance hid; for if the Gorgon dire*
> *Be shown, and thou shoudst view it, thy return*
> *Upwards would be for ever lost." This said,*

---

[12] Eliphas Levi, *The Key to the Mysteries* (York Beach, ME: Samuel Weiser, 1970 and London: Rider & Co., 1954), p. 94.

> *Himself, my gentle master, turned me round;*
> *Nor trusted he my hands, but with his own*
> *He also hid me. Ye of intellect*
> *Sound and entire, mark well the lore concealed*
> *Under close texture of the mystic strain.*[13]

Again the same myth, giving the same warning. This time is there also a reference to revenge—another attribute of Pluto? In other words, let go of the need for vengeance—blood for blood—turn the other cheek or else suffer the consequences. For, presumably, revenge in all its many forms, and the need to strike back, is also the "egoism of desire" in another disguise. Lot's wife was also told when leaving all her *possessions* (symbolic of her lower desires) in the evil cities of Sodom and Gomorrah to never look back. She did and was turned to a pillar of salt. The rewards from Pluto are great but so is the danger: Pluto is fair but his judgment is final. We are allowed to return from whence we came, stronger, with greater awareness but only on condition that the Pluto energy is used free from the egoism of desire.

What does the egoism of desire really mean? In *The Astrology of Fate*, Liz Greene speaks of something called *hubris*—understood as arrogance due to excessive pride. This, she said, was to the ancient Greeks the worst sin that man could commit. She goes on to say that the word hubris is a quality that includes not only arrogance, but vitality, nobility, heroic strivings, lack of humility before the gods, and the inevitability of a tragic end.

> When an individual is afflicted with hubris, he has attempted to overstep the boundaries of the fate set for him (which is, implicitly, the fate portrayed by the position of the heavenly bodies at birth, since the same impersonal law governs both microcosm and macrocosm). Thus he strives to become god-like; and even the gods are not permitted transgression of natural law. The core of Greek tragedy is the dilemma of hubris, which is both man's great gift and his great crime. For in pitting himself against his fated limits, he acts out a heroic destiny, yet

---

[13] Dante, *Hell,* Canto IX, lines 55-64, from *The Vision of Dante* (London: Henry Frowde, Oxford University Press, 1910).

> by the very nature of this heroic attempt he is doomed by the
> Erinyes to retribution.[14]

So is the egoism of desire the same as hubris? I think it is certainly similar.
Could it be that when we use the power of Pluto for our own personal
needs, we commit a sin and have to suffer the reverse effect of that which
we so strongly desire? In the myth of Medusa, Acrisius, King of Argos, is
warned by the oracle that he will be killed by his grandson. Because of this,
he locks up his only daughter Danaë in a prison where no one could enter,
so that she could not marry and have children. However, Zeus saw her at
her window and by changing himself into a shower of gold, he entered her
room and gave her a child which she called Perseus.

   When Acrisius found out, he was overtaken with anger and fear. He
put both mother and child in a chest and threw them into the sea so they
would drown. Zeus, however, protected the chest and led it to a distant
island called Seriphos. The inhabitants there found Danaë and her son
Perseus and led them to the king, Polydectes. He fell deeply in love with
Danaë and wanted her to himself. He became increasingly jealous as her son
Perseus grew to be a man. On the pretext of marrying another woman, he
asked Perseus for a wedding gift—the head of Medusa. He thought Perseus
would never return alive from this task, and he would have Danaë to
himself. But Hermes (the Mind of the Universe, the God of Knowledge and
Cosmic Fire, who whispers secret wisdom to the heart) suddenly appeared
to help Perseus. With his advice and help, he obtained a helmet to make him
invisible, sandals that would enable him to fly, a shield that shone like a
mirror, a sword, and a leather bag. Perseus was told not to look at Medusa's
eyes, or he would be turned to stone.

   When Perseus eventually reached Medusa, he lifted his shield which
reflected her image, enabling him to cut off her head without directly
looking at her. In some versions of the myth, Pegasus, a beautiful magical
horse, rose up from her dead body; the hero mounted the winged horse and
rode away. This story is the tale of transforming our own hidden deeper
powers, and the final reward which is freedom. But what of Polydectes who
had sought the death of the hero? When he saw Perseus, the king did not

---

[14] Liz Greene, *The Astrology of Fate* (London: Mandala, 1985 and York Beach, ME: Samuel Weiser,
1984), p. 20.

believe that the young man had slain Medusa. He told him to go away and never return. But Perseus wanted to hand over the wedding gift he had promised. Opening his bag, he lifted out the gorgon's head—her eyes were only half shut. Polydectes stared at Medusa and was immediately turned to stone.

Perseus and his mother returned home to Argos. When Danaë's father King Acrisius heard this, he remembered the prophecy and fled. The people recognized Danaë and, in time, when the king did not return, Perseus was given the throne. Acrisius lived for years as an ordinary citizen. One day he attended some athletic games in which unbeknownst to him, his grandson was competing in the discus. The discus this day was wet and slippery, and it flew out of Perseus' hands into the crowd, hitting an old man on the head. Perseus was deeply distressed as he saw the old man dying in a pool of blood. Perseus begged his forgiveness as he knelt before him and asked him who he was.

"I am Acrisius and I used to be King of Argos," the old man replied.

"But I am Perseus, Danaë's son, your grandchild!" said Perseus.

Acrisius realized he could not escape his destiny. He had hoped to be free of its laws. But destiny has its own inextricable law from which no one can escape, except by overcoming the egoism of desire.

The following example demonstrates these myths being enacted, and how the Pluto energy can be used to heal. Paula was a young married career woman in her mid-30s who was severely ill with cancer. She had been operated on twice, but each time the cancer had returned. She was on chemotherapy, very weak, and emaciated. Her chart was as remarkable as she was herself. Although I had been using imagery with cancer patients for some years, Paula gave me the first glimpse of the tremendous transpersonal healing power of the unconscious. When she was channeling this power, nothing seemed impossible.

Paula's ability to tap into and use some form of universal guidance was evident from all the easy aspects from her Sun, Mercury, and Venus in Aquarius in the 4th to Uranus in Gemini in the 8th and Neptune in Libra in the 12th. See Chart 10 on page 140. But what was also strikingly evident was all the hard aspects to her Sun and personal planets from Pluto in the 10th house. Pluto in the 10th can manifest in various ways depending on the rest of the chart. For instance, I have noticed that some people with a 10th

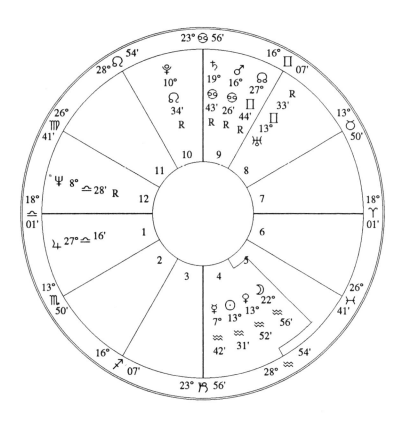

Chart 10. Paula. Birth data from family has been withheld for confidentiality. Chart calculated with Placidus Houses, using Nova/Printwheels.

house Pluto have a fear of the world overwhelming them and thus need to take power into their own hands by dominating this "world" somehow. Also a 10th house Pluto can be very overwhelmed by the parental archetypal image (I believe the mother and/or the father can be linked to the 10th). These people sometimes blame one or other parent for all their problems and refuse to accept responsibility for their own hang-ups, however well-aspected other areas connected to the mother and father image may be.

Saturn is in Cancer on Paula's 10th house cusp. It conjuncts Mars, which indicates a deep need to succeed—perhaps at the expense of deeper emotional requirements. There was much frustration present here due to the Mars-Saturn conjunction. Jupiter in the 1st house possibly gave Paula an overly optimistic attitude regarding her capabilities, and when she over-expanded due to this optimism, she was restricted by the square from Saturn to Jupiter.

Paula was a client before I started working with Saturn and Pluto, although I did use imagery. In therapy she quickly and readily took to working on an inner level, receiving guidance and help from what at the time seemed a truly divine source. She met a figure who acted as a guide, and when asked why she was ill and if she would get better he replied to her, "You attracted suffering through an exaggerated need for love and—you fear disappointments—but also aspirations. Your final outcome is to transcend both. There is an awakening of forces from your deepest depths that seek to transcend that which is overpowering. Your own desire nature will determine the outcome."

She recovered rapidly, surprising everyone including the doctors, but, as she regained her strength over a period of three or four months, her ability to work on an inner level started to fade. Its place was taken over by the need to go back into the world, to do all the things she had not been able to do when she was ill. Now this showed courage, but what has to be asked is—and this is important—was it at the expense of her own emotional needs and of something else beyond the material, as was suggested by the Uranus-Neptune placement? Her need to be a person of prominence and power in the world took precedence over all, even her own peace of mind. She wanted to do more and more, taking on more than she could cope with to satisfy the gigantic needs of a badly-aspected Pluto in Leo in the 10th house. She also became more and more dissatisfied with her emotional relationships.

Not surprisingly the cancer returned. She again worked on an inner level. Meeting her guide figure again, she asked him why the cancer had returned. He said, "You have seen your soul but there is a long way to go. If you deny your inner self it becomes ferocious—but if you obey it, it becomes benign. Raise your passions to a higher level—your qualities of innocence have become blocked. You hang on to meaningless activities to avoid the real responsibilities of life—you must rearrange your stubborn emotional approach for you are self-indulgent when restraint is needed."

Paula again made a dramatic return to wholeness and recovered her equilibrium and her health. But again she attempted too much in connection with her work and forgot many of her other needs. Again the cancer returned. She could not find the balance between her desire for material wealth, prestige, the need to succeed, and her emotional needs and the impersonal aspects in her chart pushing for transcendence and release. We can see the myth of Perseus here, but how are we to appease Plutonic energies of such prominence?

Pluto can be likened to a madness that seizes the mind and drives out reason. I'm sure we can all recognize this in some form or other. Another woman working regularly with Pluto asked him about this very problem. She had visited him many times, and he had appeared to her in many different forms. She learned to like him and went to him without any fear. She tells of her journey.

> I went down the winding steps into the dungeons. They were lit with burning torches attached to the wall. This was the only light. There were many shadows. I saw the god Pluto standing there tall, with his arms folded over his chest. He had a dark hood over his head, as he always does when I first see him. I used to be rather frightened of him, never being sure of who I would meet when he took off his hood. When I first met him, he had the head of a jackal, then on the second visit he had the head of a half-human cat. Gradually as I visited him more, this changed until he became a man. I always used to ask him if he would be my friend, but now I am so sure of his friendship, I do not need to ask. I say to him: "I have come to ask you about your energies. They seem to come from such a deep source—how can I learn to work with them more consciously?"

He takes off his hood and I see that today he looks almost like an angel. He replies, "I always work with you—I am not against you—I am always your friend. What I do, I do only for your sake. Try and be less fearful—allow more into awareness. By doing this you begin to see that which has been hidden—and thus you grow."

I give my gift to him which is a blue swan that I saw hatch in a dream; to me, it symbolized creativity. I ask him another question. "Sometimes I feel completely taken over by an energy I cannot control. It is very obsessive, I do not like it. It makes me very tense."

His reply to this is, "My energy comes from a very deep source, a source virtually unconscious. It is made up from past and present desires in this and other lives. The energy must be acknowledged: until it is, it will have an obsessive quality. Accept it as your own, *recognize the desire that created it*, love it, turn it to good use in the world."

Recognizing the desire is the key here. How many of our unconscious desires do we recognize? If, like Paula mentioned earlier, we are told from an inner source where our weaknesses lie, do we in fact recognize them within ourselves, or quickly forget what seems inconvenient to our lives and what we think we want? By working with Pluto we may begin to see some light penetrating the darkness of our own shadows. Pluto and Saturn, we must remember, are *both* lords of karma.

Sometimes it is necessary for us to enter a period of darkness within our lives, a period of gestation in order to bring to birth a new awareness within. After this birth, we are never the same again, as the entry into the darkness signifies the dissolution and death of part of ourselves, a part we have outgrown so that a new consciousness can be born. It can be lonely and frightening in the gloom, and we always have to keep in mind that this period is inevitable and necessary—just as the seasons are necessary in the fertility of nature. Spring and summer will return, as they must, with all their new growth and promise.

People who cannot, or will not, accept their own darkness and need for transformation and avoid facing the real issues connected to their own shadows, must inevitably suffer even though they have come through the darkness apparently in one piece. How do they suffer? By remaining infertile, impotent, barren of what life has to offer. They are unhappy, sometimes ill or old before their time, without trust or confidence in life. They feel as if they are blown about by the winds of chance, without hope, unable to recognize even the fertile periods of their existence. When they realize that life has not brought them the happiness they believed it would, they eventually become as frightened of life as they are of death. Frances Wickes speaks of the man who refuses the Self:

> . . .he has yielded to a regressive force which makes him content to remain less than he might become if he would give life to his own potential. Despair confronts the man who believes that he has forever lost the opportunity of becoming himself and of expressing the significance and meaning of his existence. Negation permeates his every act and an undertow of anxiety vitiates energy; guilt is generalized; hope of redemption is lost because there is no known sin to be expiated or transgression to be forgiven. Fear of life becomes fear of death because death of the spirit has already closed the door upon rebirth.

> Yet, there is always the gift of grace, for the Self, even in childhood, is showing glimpses of that other creative life-giving trinity—self-awareness, self-affirmation, self-acceptance—the three that become the four through a love of Self that opens out into a love of God in man and man in God.

> This, though a gift of grace, must be chosen and rechosen, affirmed and reaffirmed by the ego, for self-awareness grows from many choices, many acceptances of the unacceptable, many acts of loyalty to that which the Self has revealed in moments of deep experience.[15]

PLUTO AND TRANSFORMATION

When the ego identifies with the desire nature, it fears any sort of death because death threatens its existence, and so it rigorously resists the idea.

---

[15] Frances Wickes, *The Inner World of Choice*, p. 278.

Yet no one really desires the opposite of death—endless, unchanging stasis. Our spirit nature recognizes the true "key to immortality":

> Only the spiritual eye is capable of seeing stability in transfor-
> mation. Transformation is the form in which the spirit moves:
> it is life itself.... Death is the protest of the spirit against the
> unwillingness of the formed to accept transformation: the
> protest against stagnation.[16]

The tarot card connected to Scorpio, whose ruler is now generally accepted as Pluto, is card XIII, Death. The Rider-Waite pack shows a skeleton in black armor, riding a white horse and holding a banner with a white rose that is symbolic of refined and transformed passions. The King, representing the rigid ego, lies flat on the ground. The figure from the church stands, showing how our religious views and beliefs can occasionally help us over our fears of death and darkness. The young girl, representing the partly-formed ego, kneels but half turns away. Yet the child, symbolizing the Self, with all its innocence is the only one without fear and kneels offering death some flowers.

It also is interesting when examining the 13th tarot card that it is clearly reminiscent of Saturn. Older versions of the card show a skeleton holding a scythe with heads and parts of bodies lying in the grass. There is definitely some reference to Chronos here, who, you remember, eats his own children. It has already been mentioned in the Introduction how Saturn can limit the conscious mind, and Pluto the unconscious mind—so difficult transits or progressions to either of these planets will force conscious, as well as unconscious, issues to the fore, in order to be faced.

Pluto enables us to let go of old and deep habits that often lie deeply hidden in the unconscious mind. It is common when people are going through heavy Pluto transits or progressions that they behave in a way quite alien to them. This initially can be quite frightening but also very liberating in the long term. When experiencing these transits people often find themselves saying things they would never have said before—breaking down emotional barriers, letting out hidden jealousies and resentments of long duration. The more rigidly the ego is in service to the lower desires—and the greater the resistance—the more powerful can be the release. It is

---

[16] Lama A. Govinda, *Foundations of Tibetan Mysticism* (Farmington: CT, 1987), pp. 219, 220.

certain, however, that by genuinely trying to work with and not against the Pluto energy, much good can be achieved. The energy is impersonal and only seeks release into new and productive channels. To try to stop this happening is like damming up a river when it is flooding: it has to find the weakest point of resistance and then break through. Those that try to hang on to past actions and reactions live in the quagmire of yesterday's dammed up river—their own habits—bogged down in the mud in the midst of life, experiencing lethargy, depression and often illness, as well as many inner terrors.

It is interesting when working with people to find the differences among them regarding their acceptance or resistance to new growth during Pluto transits or progressions. Some people willingly work to free themselves, eager to explore their darker sides, while others hesitate, although showing some interest; others are entirely unaware of what is going on inside, unconscious of their own needs, as well as the needs of those around them. It is as if there really is a dark veil between them and their inner being. Resistance to the energy can result in illness—permanent or transitory—mental or physical. The psychological structure of the personality and the person's age are also important. The energy can also be released through other people—a happening in the outer world—a marriage breakup—an accident—a death—but ultimately it is a sign which says, "Where do you fit in with all of this, and what can you learn from it about yourself?"

I remember a patient whose husband died suddenly in his early 40s. Her chart shows a Mars-Pluto progressed opposition (4th and 10th house), plus transiting Pluto square both Mars and Pluto and square her 7th house Sun. Venus and Mercury were also in the 7th. She had given everything to her home life, often at the expense of herself and had always put her husband and his career first, without thinking of herself or her own needs. There was also a teenage daughter and two sons who were being educated at private schools, which, since they lived at home, necessitated much fetching and carrying.

When he died, this client was utterly lost and existed on tranquilizers and help from her family for the first year or two, totally unable to cope alone. Finally she decided to try therapy for, as she said, she could not go on this way much longer. She had been married at an early age and had spent the first few married years helping her husband up the ladder of success. He had paid all the bills and arranged everything. He had decided when they would move to new and larger houses and made all decisions that affected their lives together. When I suggested the chart showed that she had a lot of inner strength she denied this, saying she could never manage on her own. But during the next few months of therapy, it became apparent even to her that she did have a great deal of strength and integrity that she had never developed, as her husband had always been the strong one and done everything for her.

After a year of therapy she appeared strong, confident, and sure of herself, and managed all her household affairs with ease. She moved to a smaller house, which was more suitable to her needs and began a small business which became successful, but she kept it small, because it suited her that way. She met a widower of whom she became very fond. He, in time, asked her to marry him. She initially declined his offer for, as she confessed, her life was now very happy and complete. But with three planets in the 7th house, partnerships are important, and so she eventually agreed on the condition that she could stay independent, and that the marriage would be a joint partnership in which each shared and worked together. I met her again after she had been married for about three years: she told me how happy she was, admitting that she was far happier now than she had ever been before. But it had taken a terrible tragedy for her to be able to find herself. Perhaps all these things are planned; perhaps we are all just actors waiting to play our parts on stage. But in any case, we must face that which we fear in order to redeem something of value from within ourselves.

How much is predestined, and how much free will do we have? It seems evident that we are all given certain tasks to complete in life. We all have to go through periods of learning, but having said that, I do believe we have free will, although admittedly this free will is very difficult to attain.

Past desires form our present karma. As long as we desire, karma will always be created. So you could say, if we stop desiring, this will solve the problem. The answer to this is both yes and no. If we stop desiring because we wish to avoid future karma, it cannot work. But if we realize that at specific points in life, we are, due to astrological influences brought about by previous karma, going to desire something, then we can *will* not to oppose these energies, but endeavor to work with them and transcend them by union with the Self—thus working in harmony with natural law.

Obviously the more you can understand yourself on the deepest levels the better. But however much you understand yourself, unless you can unite with the Self you cannot ever rise above or conquer your desire nature. Understanding the various parts of our natures is the first step in uniting with the Self, but until the egoism of desire is released, the Self can never manifest. This is Pluto's lesson—this is also free will.

PLUTO AND LIBERATION OF SELF

The wind you have made free,
Therefore it lightly obeys your commands;
But me you have loaded with burdens,
With them I toil on.
Passing from death to death,
Slowly I free myself from them,
Till empty-handed I come
Ready to serve you. [17]

All aspects to Pluto need careful study and analysis. Planets aspecting Pluto will increase in nature and intensity in either a positive or negative way. Pluto-Moon will bring a greater intensity of emotional feeling—if channeled well, this can be tremendously creative; at its worst, tremendously destructive. Pluto-Mercury will give more power in speech and communications. It can persuade, manipulate, and control in these areas—both in oneself and others—but it can also become a channel to help achieve deeper understanding when the control element is released. Pluto-Venus deepens the relating principal, often in connection with the love life. It is always intense in its relating: this can be in the form of extreme loyalty and dedication or extreme possessiveness and jealousy with a strong need to control. Pluto will add vitality when in aspect to the Sun which can create an active dynamism or a need to always be in charge. Pluto will also bring the same intensity to the house or sign it occupies.

Progressions and transits from Pluto can be very liberating, in the long term, to those willing to work with them. But for those people who live life

---

[17] Rabindraneth Tagore, *A Flight of Swans* (London: John Murrey, 1955), p. 28.

very *unconsciously*, the harder aspects can be difficult. I have seen strong men and women, who have come through the toughest assignments, go to pieces when in the grips of a hard Pluto transit. Although the more flowing transits give liberation with less intensity and fewer obsessional impulses, they will always generate an energy that forces hidden aspects of ourselves to the surface. In individuals who have a trace of mental instability, Pluto transits can often trigger psychotic disturbances, particularly when linked to the Moon. It seems in these cases there is often not much we can do but give support until the time passes. The majority of people, however, can choose to work with the god of the nether regions, try to understand his message, and receive his gift when he departs—for there is always a gift to be found if we choose to look for it.

• • •

Kate, mentioned earlier, had spent her life helping others at the complete expense of herself and her peace of mind. After working with Saturn she went to Pluto to ask for help with her problem. She has Pluto in Leo squaring her Scorpio Ascendant and Saturn and Jupiter in Taurus. See Chart 9 on page 72.

The wood is very dark.
I go down in the lift.
Then down the stairs.
I see someone standing there.
I feel frightened—but safe also.
My gift is a sincere wish to work through my darker side.
I give it in the form of a wreath made in the shape of a heart.

Someone steps from the shadows.
I see Pluto now—he is a dark angel.
I am not sure of my feelings towards him.

I ask my question.
"I want relief from my depression
which I believe is caused by an unconscious block somewhere."

Pluto speaks to me: It is caused through a block.
And it is time you looked at it in detail.

Accept darkness—do not be afraid.
It will only hurt you if you allow it.
You need to bring love
and warmth to your own darkness.
It can be a good place—where you learn to grow.

We look in the cages.
First cage—all I see is a blob.
No, it is a dark figure cowering in the corner.
It is a human figure with burning aggressive eyes.
I feel rather afraid.
It is Hate.

Second cage—a lonely woman.
She has a very sad feeling.
She has very little to live for.
She is lonely because she has had to work
through much responsibility.
She cannot be happy
and accept the good things in life.

Third cage—a figure with red, staring eyes.
I feel frightened.
This is fear.

Fourth cage—the cage is empty but seems to be full of warmth.

Fifth cage—it seems that the Sun is in this cage.
Everywhere is full of light.
It is calm and peaceful.
It smells sweet.
I think it is the "Whole" as it is meant to be.
There is strength there.
Kind gentle strength.
And all the love available.

I become Pluto.

I see Kate as unhappy, beaten,
unable to pick up,

discouraged and disillusioned.
I do not like to see her so trapped.

We decide to let out the lonely woman from the first cage. She needs company, help, and support. She is sensitive and nervous but glad to be out. She goes up the stairs, all the time becoming happier. She finds a friend she has been looking for and sits down happily. She will be all right now.

We also open the cage with the Sun in. It shines in every corner of the cell. It makes everything very beautiful. It seems to shine in Kate's heart. She is more "whole" now than she has been for a long time.

I leave the other cages.

I become Kate again.

Pluto says, "Never be afraid.
Never fear or worry, just *be*."

The second visit to Pluto is made a few weeks later.

I see Pluto; he is very big.
He is beautiful in a strange way.
He has lots of dark hair
And a very white face with dark eyes.
I wonder if his face is so white
because he never sees the Sun.

Today I feel much more positive.
I give a knife to Pluto as my gift.
It is two-edged,
Representing sharpness with kindness.
He is pleased with the gift.

We go over to the cages.
I am reluctant to look but not frightened.

First cage—Hate is there—he seems very big.
He seems more like a blob again

and less like a man.
He is quivering and crawling.
I understand now why he became this way—
it is through jealousy.
I want to help him
but I do not know in what way.
And I can't help feeling
a repugnance when I look at him.
He unnerves me.

Second cage—this cage is empty but full of warmth.
The lonely woman has left.
She is no longer lonely.
She is making a new life for herself.
There is a vase of beautiful flowers on the floor.
Almost in reverence to her departure.

Third cage—Fear is still here looking rather pitiful.
He is almost like a human skeleton.
But his eyes are not so red and staring today.
I feel so sorry for him.
His fear starves him and stops him receiving help.

Fourth cage—this cage is still empty.
It still feels warm.
I am not sure what it represents.
It may be warm memories that keep me going.
Or kindnesses that are shown to me by others.
I begin to understand now.
I never let others help me.
"This" is what it means.
It feels nice to be here.
Soon I will open this cage.
But not today.
I am not quite ready yet.
Pluto nods in approval,
pleased that I have at last recognized
the contents of this cell.

Fifth cage—this cage is still full of sunlight.
It is beautiful.
There is such gentle strength here still.

Cages one and three seem to need a lot of help. We decide the occupants there are not yet ready to be given their freedom. I realize what they need is some of the sunlight. I ask Pluto if we can bring the Sun into the other cages.

He nods in approval and says, "Yes, at last you see the answer. But you must help."

We concentrate on the Sun in cage five.
I ask that it will radiate out and fill the other cages.
Gradually the Sun becomes more and more powerful.
It radiates into all the other cages.
A feeling of hope and love spreads out.
I know everything will soon be all right.

I become Pluto.
I feel big—dark—and part of the darkness.
The darkness is friendly.
Kate is looking lighter and brighter in some way.
I see she is much happier and younger also—
and I am glad.

I become Kate again.

Pluto looks warm and smiling.
I realize the Sun does shine here.
And that the darkness makes it even brighter.
I feel Pluto is a friend.

I am no longer ashamed of feeling fearful, hateful, and jealous. Soon I will accept others' kindnesses towards me and let them help. And I'll love all those parts of me until they heal and I no longer need to keep them locked up.

So it seems that we have to begin to accept and understand our own darkness with the deepest sincerity, before we can conceive the greater significance of what the Lord of death has to offer us. He ultimately offers us liberation from that which previously had been our prison.

• • •

The following two examples of working with Pluto are Robert's experiences. He has Pluto in Cancer in the 11th house trining a Pisces Sun in the 8th, and Pisces Moon in the 7th. Pluto conjuncts Mars and Jupiter in Cancer in the 11th and opposes Saturn in Capricorn in the 5th. Pluto also squares Uranus in Aries in the 8th, and semi-squares Neptune on his Virgo Ascendant. He had worked with Pluto on several occasions previously. See Chart 6 on page 56.

> My gift to Pluto is my sincere commitment to liberty and the shadow side—I give this symbolically to Pluto in the form of a four-inch black marble cube.
>
> My Question is of "woman" and my sexuality.
>
> Pluto weighs the gift and is satisfied—even agreeably impressed in a mild way.
>
> I say I want to truly *accept* my sexuality and understand it—and I feel the answer is down here.
>
> Pluto replies, "Yes, the answer is down here. Have no fear, I will make sure no barrier is further in your way to free yourself from false suffering. A long, long time in the making—a relatively short time in release."
>
> I look into the cages.
>
> First cage—the figure has very long hair and straggly beard—reminiscent of Robinson Crusoe—he seems quite "mad"—in an abstracted sort of way. He is bound by insecurity and has not the confidence to leave his cell—though he has only to ask. I tell him I want to be his friend, that help is near at hand. I ask him if there is anything he wants.
>
> He says, "Yes, I want to leave here but I don't know where to go."

I say, "Soon I will take you somewhere else—and then I will look after you."

"Good," says Pluto, "you are taking responsibility and recognizing him at last—it is not that difficult you know—all that is needed is strength of will. In the past you have taken responsibility for the wrong things in the wrong way, without knowing what you were doing. Now you make a start at being sensible. Good, I like it. Know me and you know your salvation."

I feel a certain excitement, joy and hope in what I see already— and confidence—for I do see that what is needed is my acknowledgment and acceptance—not a herculean effort.

Second cage—a voice says, "Look not at him, look at us—we're the tough ones." Anger said this—he has been standing at the bars of his cage looking out—the cage he shares with Depression. Depression is sitting at the table holding a cup—a cup that Anger and Depression had formerly fought over.

Anger says, "Oh what the hell—he needs it so I gave it to him."

I said, "But why?"

"Because I can get what I want—he can't stand up for himself— he needs something to build himself up. When I get out of here, nobody is going to walk over me and piss me about—and I will get out. I know you need me—and what's more I know you know you need me."

"Well what are you going to do about him?" I ask.

"What are *you* going to do about him you mean?" Anger says.

"Well you can stop him getting walked over can't you—and you'd like that?" I say.

"*There* is your strength," Pluto says. "He is not just anger. Anger is frustrated strength. Now at last you begin to see not just the anger." It is true. There has been *such* a change here. And this, too, fills me with hope.

Third cage—this cage is empty except for a small bird—a sparrow that is flying about as though it cannot get out.

"What does it mean Pluto?"

"It means he can't get out," Pluto says.

"But there is space enough."

"Yes but he does not think so," Pluto replies. "He does not see it."

"You mean he is blind?"

"No, he's panicking, so his fear distorts his judgment."

At this point the sparrow comes and sits on a cross-piece of the grid bar.

And I say, "It's all right, just fly out," and this it does. Now it is empty.

I say "Who was that?"

Pluto says, "That was the spirit of a time past."

Fourth cage—I'm beginning to feel quite tired now—and this is the cell with the problem.

Pluto says, "Just relax; you don't have to do anything; just be here."

There are women in the cage, their backs are toward me—the cage is light and between them and me is a veil.

I am told, "There is no mystery, the veil is your own fear of us. You see in us what you, yourself, project. And we are no mystery. You do not recognize us—who we are. What are we?"

I ask them, "All right who are you?"

They say "We are you—that part of you that you almost never knew. Now go gently, hear the moan of those rejected: listen to what they say— and remember, we love you."

After all this I say, "Even so."

"And what are we but your female side, your creativity—for without us you are as dead. Fear not your way is clear. But let us have more light. Let us serve the gifts that Mother Nature bestowed. Create and free your fellow man. Accept us as we are. That is the secret. Resonate."

I say, "Thank-you, I will respond. Restore you to your proper places."

Pluto adds, "There are such gifts bestowed here as will transform your life. Work that *they* may be justified."

This is not what I expected—what I thought would be an insurmountable problem has seemingly dissolved. I feel as if a great burden has been lifted. Pluto puts his arm around my shoulder in a reassuring way and says, "There," as much as to say, "That is over."

When I become Pluto I feel very solid and together. I see myself dressed as a Knight Templar, his head radiant. We open cages three and four. The females are delighted to be in the hall, and dance for joy. They are obviously thrilled. The bird flies happily around the hall—eventually flying out through the window—where he joins a group of sparrows that all fly off together.

I become myself again. Pluto says, "You are always welcome here."

A month later another visit is made to Pluto—this time to ask about death.

Pluto says, "Yes, yet again dear friend—for so you are—we work to make yourself whole, in the ground of your personality; yourself and your actions—for so it is to be. No suffering now. Work for the wholeness of mankind. Let us begin."

My gift to Pluto is a crystal sphere—which symbolizes the light—and is itself from the earth.

Pluto takes it, playing with it like a toy—throwing it up in the air with his left hand and catching it. He intentionally lets it fall to the ground. On hitting the ground it smashes into a thousand pieces.

I am unnerved by this occurrence—it isn't what I expected. Pluto reaches his hand to the ground. His fingers—or hand— have a magnetic effect on the fragments which re-collect themselves into the sphere as his hand reaches the ground. And he picks it up, saying, "And so it is with you—the crystal sphere of light (spirit). Here you come to re-collect the lost bits in the (shadow) darkness to make yourself whole. It is only your willingness that can do this. The trust—the desire to be whatever—however blemished—Rock Crystal.

I feel a gratitude—a joy in his company.

I explain to him that I wish to know more of death and also wish to continue work on the cages.

Pluto asks, "Why do you come to me to ask about death?"

"Because this is your domain," I reply.

Pluto says, "Very well. Death is a transformation. Death is just another image. You pass from one image to another. The passing is death. It has its morphology. Its beginning, its middle, its end. Its moment—or rather it is a moment. Its approach is now. Its departure is now. But "it" is not now—Like sleep— From one dream to another, (through sleep) losing consciousness. A moment of stop. Of suspended animation. Death is a door. Close the door. Open the door. There is no death. Death is a dream. As shadows in the light. Death is breathing in. Death is breathing out. Death is departure. Death is arrival. Death is the journey. The unknown journey. Death is the journey of transformation. Death is the journey into life. Death brings you here. There is no death, only departures. Yes, you experience a million deaths. Enough! you are tiring. Why not let us look at the cells."

The cages show the following:

First cage—the Robinson Crusoe figure is sitting at a table playing patience. He is clean, cheerful, wearing a white shirt.

His spirits are high. He is feeling a lot better. But is clearly nervous of contact with others.

Second cage—the cage is dark—no one there—Anger and Depression gone. Then I see a rather gaunt figure staring at me through the bars. This is Fear their brother.

Third cage—this cage is light. There is only a snake moving on the floor.

Fourth cage—this is empty—no one there.

Fifth cage—there is a figure sitting in an attitude of despair. I thought I might recognize him but I didn't. I ask him who he is: he says "Guilt."

I realize at this point I am feeling quite good on the whole—although cells two and five obviously need attention. I feel very close to Pluto. I become him. There is a solid sensation. I see myself as more grown up.

We decide cages one, two and, three can wait—but five should be let out. The dungeon can only compound its despair and guilt. I see the figure now seems to have a female aspect. This woman, as she proceeds up the stairs to the hall, gathers herself together—putting on a brave face. And although anxiously tense, she makes an effort to join in, finally sitting down and relaxing. She sees there is no danger—that she is accepted.

I become myself again. Pluto says, "Come again when you need to."

We can see from the above experiences that Pluto in his role as Lord of Darkness is also a Lord of Light. By working with Pluto, we can let go of old habits and thought patterns, which have created burdens for us in this lifetime, as well as karma we have perpetuated in previous existences. Pluto will work with us but asks for a commitment that is not to be taken lightly. He often warns visitors to his domain that in order to help he must have total sincerity—that his powers should not be used for personal gain or self-aggrandizement.

Pluto once said: "I am the dark angel on the threshold that is locked away beyond time. The keys I hold unlock mysteries even beyond your imagination or understanding. I am the Alpha and Omega, the black and white. I am the avenging angel—and the dark rider. Also I am light immortal—the flame of the living flame. I *am* retribution—but also release. I am Pluto."

The Pluto Meditation

The Pluto Meditation enables us to let go of old and outworn thought and habit patterns as well as those parts of us that are ready to go on to new experiences. Before this can happen, however, it is necessary that the responsibilities exacted by Saturn be faced. By working with Pluto we are recognizing and releasing those parts of us that require a new birth, a new way to be. The following list will summarize the various benefits and experiences you may have while working with the Pluto meditation technique.

1) During heavy transits or progressions, use when needed. It has been noted how, during a Pluto transit, the energy sometimes builds up to an unbearable level. By using this Meditation, not only do you begin to work through problems on a deep inner level, but you also experience some relief from Pluto's obsessional and oppressive energies (which only need to be recognized).

2) Any feeling of fear attached to Pluto and the underworld quickly dispels after a few meetings. It is only your own darkness you fear. As I was told by Pluto, "It is only goodness untransformed." No one has ever reported Pluto as being unkind. In fact, he appears quite the reverse.

3) The gift to Pluto can be something you wish to work through, or something you wish to share with him. Sometimes the gift is symbolic, and you are not always sure of its meaning at the time.

4) The cages represent "locked-up" parts of your nature that require attention. In the cages can be found persons or scenes, or any animate or inanimate object.

5)   When looking in the cages it is important to recognize what the contents signify in your life. If you do not understand their meaning, work on this by doing the following: ask Pluto if he understands what the contents of the cages mean; Listen and note his reply. If he cannot help you, leave the cages locked. Write down, in as much detail as possible, what is in the cages. In the next few days, see if any interpretations occur to you. To understand the images fully, you need to keep working with them until you recognize the meaning. For only then can you *truly* release what is there.

6)   When the cages become empty, they still contain a living quality and will continue to contain (at certain times) what you need to accept, understand, and eventually release. Even though you have dealt with what was originally there, this does not mean the cage is finished with forever. The cages may also vary in number at different visits.

7)   When you work with Pluto, you are taking charge of your own karma— positive or negative—with the choice of opening the cages or not.

8)   The hall upstairs represents "your world." What you release from the cages, then, becomes integrated into this world—or is released to go beyond.

9)   There is always a sense of relief after the experience—it cannot be put into words—it is just there. However, the first visit or two that is ever made to Pluto can sometimes leave a drained feeling. But as you get used to working this way, it soon goes.

10) To do the Meditation, sit or lie down in a comfortable position and thoroughly relax.

11) For any of the meditations to work, it is necessary to be deeply committed to the exercise. This way you will derive the most understanding and lasting benefit from them.

AN EXAMPLE OF PLUTO MEDITATION.

Imagine you are standing in a very dark wood.
It is nighttime. The moon is bright.

There are huge old trees all around you.
You can see the shapes of the trees.
You notice how very large they are.
The tree you are standing near,
one of the largest of them all,
has an opening in it as large as a doorway.
You enter into this tree.
When inside, you see through the darkness
a door which you open.
You now realize the door is a door into an elevator.
You know this is where you want to go.
You go through the door into the elevator,
closing the door behind you.

As you do this, the elevator starts to move downwards.
You go down and down, deeper, deeper,
and deeper into the earth.
Down and down, down and down.
Deeper and deeper, deeper and deeper.
You pass the first level and the second and third level.
The fourth and the fifth level slide by.
The sixth, seventh, and eighth.
Eventually, the elevator shudders to a halt.
The gate automatically opens for you.
You find yourself standing in a part of a very old castle.
You see huge stone walls rising up above you.
There are torches alight on the wall
throwing eerie shadows.
All you can really see are steps going downwards.
It seems to be the only place to go.
So you go down the steps which circle round.
Take care as they are quite steep in places.
As you go down
the steps go round and round and down.
When you reach the bottom of the steps,
you find yourself at the very bottom of the castle.
You realize this is where the dungeons are.

Imagine you are standing in a very dark wood. It is nighttime. The moon is bright. There are huge old trees all around you. You can see the shapes of the trees. You notice how very large they are. The tree you are standing near, one of the largest of them all, has an opening in it as large as a doorway.

You see a vast area supported by huge stone pillars.
You see torches on the wall and many shadows,
And what you take to be cages set around in the walls.
You walk along and you see a figure
standing there waiting for you.
A man with his arms folded
wearing a black hood over his head.
You walk up to him.
And say to him, "Will you work with me and be my friend?"
And he will take off his mask and answer you.
Listen to his words.

Imagine you have brought a gift for him.
A gift appropriate to him.
For he is the god of the underworld.
(Sometimes the god may take on a female form).
Give him the gift.
How do you see the person before you?
How do you feel about him?
He will ask you why you are there and what you want.
Tell him.
Listen carefully to the reply.

Then walk over to the dungeons with the god.
How many dungeons do you see?
Look in each one and note what is in there.
Note how you feel as you look at each different cage.

Now, again, observe the person standing before you,
the jailer.
The supreme one of the underworld.
How does this person look to you?
How does this person stand?
How do you feel about him?

Then step out of yourself and into the jailer—
the ruler of the underworld.
Get right into his body.

You find yourself standing in a part of a very old castle. You see huge stone walls rising up above you. There are torches alight on the wall throwing eerie shadows. All you can really see are steps going downwards. It seems to be the only place to go. So you go down the steps which circle round. Take care as they are quite steep in places.

Hold your arms and hands in the same way.
See how the head feels.
Then turn and look at yourself.
How do you see yourself—
and do you like what you see?

Go to one cage at a time.
Both agree as to whether what is there
can be released—
this is important.
Then take the large key which hangs at your belt
and open the cages you have agreed upon.
You can open one or more cages now.
Or, if you choose,
come back another time and open cages.
But let out that which you think is safe
to let out at this moment now.
If you have any doubts or worries at this time,
keep the cages locked.
There will be another staircase in the dungeons
and everything you let out today
will go up this second staircase—
to the part of the castle where people live.
As they go upwards follow—see what happens.
At the top of the stairs
will be a huge banquet hall.
Notice how the occupants of the cages
behave now they are released.
Remember you are still the ruler of the underworld.
When you have noted everything,
walk back down the staircase
with the part of you which is yourself.
Back to the dungeons.
When you reach them stand outside
and step back into yourself.
Into your own body again.
Check the empty dungeons.

You find yourself at the very bottom of the castle. You realize this is where the dungeons are. You see a vast area supported by huge stone pillars. You see torches on the wall and many shadows, and what you take to be cages set around in the walls. You walk along and you see a figure standing there waiting for you.

Are they completely empty?
Thank the ruler of the underworld
for all the help which has been given you.
Ask if you may come again—
listen to his reply.
Find the first staircase again.
Walk up this staircase to the elevator.
Enter in the elevator—
the door will close behind you.
The elevator will rise up
through the different levels
until you reach the earth level again.
And will come to stop in the tree in the forest.
The gate will open
and you will walk back onto the earth again.
Then very gently in your own time
let your consciousness come back into your own room.
And again in your own time open your eyes.

APPENDICES

Appendix I: Questions and Answers

Question: What is the best way to use the Saturn Meditation when you are having difficulty with another person, *e.g.*, partner, child or work-mate?

Answer: When you go in the hall in Saturn's temple imagine that person is there—experience the negative energies between you. Then become the god and feel your full authority and strength and you will see the other person in a different way—and usually with a great deal of compassion. If there is great difficulty between you, you will have to work very hard to experience your greatness. It is only by experiencing your own true strength that you can see the reality of the situation.

Question: Will you always receive the truth—or can you sometimes be led astray?

Answer: It is important to be careful about what you are "seeing." The answer must be in the interpretation. If you avoid taking responsibility because you want instant satisfaction—or an easy way out of a difficult problem—you may be disappointed.

Question: So if I am seeing people through the eyes of Saturn, am I seeing them as they really are?

Answer: You are only seeing them through your own reality, not how they will affect others. It is a purely personal realization.

Question: Do we have a choice about how we act upon what we are given in the Saturn Meditation—or is how we behave predestined?

Answer: If you want a quick and easy solution: an instant answer—or instant gratification and are not working through the problem with *responsibility*—not experiencing your own strength and perhaps looking for the line of least resistance, you may not receive what you require; but inevitably you have to pay for the lack of responsibility at a later date—that is destiny.

Question: You speak of working through marriage problems. Do you think it's wrong to separate or get divorced? (By marriage we mean a life partner, legally recognized or otherwise.)

Answer: Read Steinbrecher's *Inner Guide Meditation* on Shadow Dancing.[1] This is an excellent interpretation of what marriage is about. He describes marriage as a partnership for two people to come together—regardless of gender—to remain together willingly, to help each other achieve consciousness and to remain sexually faithful to one another. He says marriage forms a container around the two people involved, and that sex outside that container makes leaks in the transformation vessel known as "marriage." And if you have leaks, neither of the partners can change or transform. Marriage is two people coming together and agreeing to help each other through the process of rebirth, so both achieve spiritual transformation.

Most religions wisely emphasize the sanctity of marriage. It is a partnership conceived on a deep spiritual basis so that each may become more conscious. Thus it cannot easily be dismissed. Francis Wickes' insight on the subject of divorce is also very helpful.

> . . .The outer law must not be broken except at the command of a more searching inner law, which cannot speak with authority unless, in integrity and truth, every effort has been made to fulfill the old. This effort requires a painful self-searching in order to discover the causes that have long been accumulating in the unconscious, for it is the slowly developing inner situation—not a sudden infatuation or discovery of unexpected difficulties—that produces divorce.[2]

---

[1] Edwin Steinbrecher, *The Inner Guide Meditation*, p. 137.
[2] Frances Wickes, *The Inner World of Choice*, p. 268.

Question: You are suggesting that we learn to trust the Self more, but there are people on a "spiritual path" for whom this self-trust seems a negative rather than a positive force.

Answer: Everyone needs more knowledge of Self to come through the illusions of life. Many illusions abound regarding the right spiritual path to take, but these come from the human nature and are not a true representation of the Self.

Question: So how do I know that the Self is in charge?

Answer: The Self does not manipulate or blame others, and is not afraid to take its own pathway. The Self is there at that moment when you have trust in the Universal Will. (This must never be mistaken for a pseudo-spirituality that is so common today.) It is there when you want *nothing*—but will accept that which is your lot with courage and grace. It is there at that moment when you can put every trial or pleasure or problem to good use and in service to the Lords of Light and Life and Love. And the more you understand yourself on the deepest of levels, the more the Self is able to manifest in all its purity and wisdom and thus able to begin to reach beyond the illusions of life. It must be remembered the Self is a point of awareness that is there when the Higher Mind receives guidance from the Soul. We need to constantly strive to reach that point. The more we do this, the stronger that point of awareness—that is the Self—becomes.

Question: What type of person will benefit most from the meditation?

Answer: Those with a positive active imagination, a desire for knowledge and truth, who have their feet planted firmly on the ground!

Question: Is either the Saturn or Pluto Meditation dangerous?

Answer: There are people for whom I think it would be dangerous, for instance, for people with any degree of psychotic illness, or who are heavy drug users, prescribed or otherwise. These people would benefit more from other forms of psychotherapy before attempting this exercise. (A person classified as psychotic should never attempt or be encouraged to do this type of work.)

Question: How do you feel about spiritualists and their guides?

Answer: Some time ago, I had a client who was a spiritualist medium. She was suffering a terminal illness and sought some cure. I had seen her working as a trance medium, bringing material of a positive—and as far as one could tell—genuine nature to those present. She also worked as a healer and while doing this, tuned into *something* that could only be described as highly suspicious. When working with her as a patient and trying to take her to the inner levels, she would immediately be taken over by an entity—which seemed no more than a highly dominant subpersonality—who would dictate throughout the whole session. We made no progress because this entity would make no allowances or concessions. This woman's inspired nature could only be tapped into while she was unconscious. Her lower nature personality (for this is what the other was) blocked further progress. She would accept no responsibility whatsoever for her present state of health or affairs, as she was completely convinced as to the genuineness of all the entities that came through her; she was totally in their power. I do not have a copy of her chart, but remember that she had Sun and Mercury in Cancer, trining Uranus, and Venus conjunct Pluto.

So what do I think about spiritualists and clairvoyants? I think there are some people who can tap consciously into a source of universal awareness but only through their own impersonal consciousness. Sometimes clairvoyants will bring through an inspired and genuine message and at the same time something that comes from their personal consciousness. It is rarely "pure" unless the people concerned are free from personal bias. What spiritualists often take for a guide is often no more than a part of their desire nature (cf., chapters on subpersonalities).

Question: How do I work through a severe depression?

Answer: There are several methods of tackling this situation. If you are not seeing a therapist, help yourself with Bach Flower Remedies or other flower essence therapies: gorse (hopelessness and despair), gentian (depression of a known origin), mustard (dark cloud that descends for no known reason), sweet chestnut (absolute dejection).[3]

---

[3] For addresses where you can obtain more information about or purchase the Bach Flower Remedies, see Resources, page 187.

After this initial support, which will help greatly, start tackling the cause of the depression. Depression means to depress something, to hold something down—the opposite of recognizing something within that needs to come to awareness. Read Liz Greene's *Saturn: A New Look at an Old Devil*,[4] and thoroughly investigate how the Saturn energy is affecting you. Also trace what transits and progressions you have affecting your natal chart at that time.

At this point, you should begin to recognize where some of your fears and despondencies lie. You will start to unearth the root cause of what is making you depressed and see that any fear or sense of limitation is coming from within you. Take and work with the Saturn Meditation with the support of a valuable friend or sympathetic counselor if possible.

Question: How can I stop going to sleep when I do the meditation?

Answer: Try to find out what is making you want to sleep—are you trying to avoid the Meditation? Are you afraid of it? If so, try playing the tape through when you are doing something else—like washing up or weeding the garden—get used to it and overcome your avoidance. If you are falling asleep because you are simply overtired, play the tape at some other time in the day when you have more energy and are more alert.

Question: But isn't all this introspection rather self-indulgent? Can you change human character and smother undesirable factors? Isn't it arrogant to attempt to try?

Answer: I think you may have misunderstood the aim of the exercise. All self-knowledge or knowledge of Self can be utilized wisely and constructively for the benefit of all, rather than to make oneself more important or for self-approbation. Can you change human character? The answer I think is that you can become more responsible for yourself and your actions if you choose. Some are not prepared, perhaps not equipped, to assume this way of thinking, but many of us have the ability to attain more freedom of choice than we already have. You also talk about smothering undesirable factors; this is not how it is done. We need to look at and identify with what is

---

[4] Published by London: Arkana, 1976; and York Beach, ME: Samuel Weiser, 1990

making us depressed, pessimistic, or unhappy, and to see what part of us is being affected—more than anything we need to accept what we find and learn to regard it in the future.

Question: It is all very well to say be responsible for yourself, but what about all the evil in the world?

Answer: You have to define what you mean by evil. Perhaps evil is just being unconsciously motivated by distortions within the personality, such as fear, greed, gossip, intolerance, resentment, jealousy, and manipulation. Many things cause evil, and yet often these evil actions are perpetrated entirely unconsciously, by ourselves as well as others. Therefore, if these are the things on which evil is built, we can see all evil as a lesson in self-understanding.

Question: What if I become afraid while using the Saturn or Pluto Meditation?

Answer: Define what you are afraid of. Is it Saturn or Pluto, and if so, why? Try and write down why. Is it because it's the first time you have used the tape? If this is the case, play the tape through while you are doing something else like housework or gardening. This way you will see there is nothing there to harm you—and only to help you. (Never play it in a moving vehicle.) Is it because you are afraid to do the Meditation alone, particularly the first time? Then try and find a friend who will sit with you while you go through it. Is it because you meditate in a dark room? Then meditate with the lights on in a house that has other people in it. Once you have broken through your fear barrier there is no problem—and I know *no one* who has ever been frightened of the meditations after the initial breakthrough.

   If for any reason the fear persists, the Bach Flower remedies can be very helpful: aspen (for apprehensions of an unknown origin), mimulus (for fears of a known origin), rock rose (for panic and terror). If you are a *very* fearful person by nature, it may be that a therapist could help you work through some of your problems.

Question: Can you say something about what you mean by positive shadow projection?

Answer: Our shadow side may be as much positive as negative. Sometimes patients say: "My husband (or wife) is so wonderful," and then they list all their partner's positive qualities. My reply to this would be, "But that is your own shadow side you're seeing, and all those positive qualities are yours, although at the moment you only recognize them in your partner."

Question: Do you think you are playing down Saturn's negative and destructive force?

Answer: All the planets have positive and negative poles. Saturn represents responsibility to ourselves and others, strength and moral obligations— our own inner morals, not society's. When we allow these forces to oppress us instead of working with them, they become weaknesses and limitations, leading to despondency and dejection—a heaviness of spirit. For someone locked in apathy and depression, experiencing fear and anxiety, it can be a nightmare, leaving a heavy and oppressed heart. I have found, however, that when patients experience these conditions, under-standing the natal placement of Saturn and stressing and working with the positive elements helps them understand the reason their problems came about in the first place. So try to find the origin of your dissatisfaction and unhappiness, see how you can transform this particular energy. Look at what is making you unhappy with some curiosity. Why is it making you unhappy? What part of you is being affected by it? If you work sincerely, your view of things inevitably starts to change. Blavatsky in *The Voice of the Silence*, says:

> Remember, thou that fightest for man's liberation, each failure is success, and each sincere attempt wins its reward in time. The holy germs that sprout and grow unseen in the disciple's soul, their stalks wax strong at each new trial, they bend like reeds but never break, nor can they e'er be lost. But when the hour has struck they blossom forth.[5]

Question: Is it wrong and irresponsible to be homosexual?

---

[5] Madame H. P. Blavatsky, *The Voice of the Silence* (Pasadena, CA: Theosophical University Press, 1971), p. 63.

Answer: When talking of homosexuality, is it the sexual act you are talking about, or an ongoing relationship between two people of the same sex? Sex is just a part of any relationship—to some, a very important part, to others less so. If two people can develop between them a loving, caring, responsible way of life, helping each other to grow as human beings, what can be wrong if it leads to the mutual growth of those concerned—the growth of love, compassion, sharing, kindness, and other positive qualities?

Question: If we become whole and strong, can we do without close relationships?

Answer: If we become more whole and strong, admittedly we are not perhaps so dependent on others, so the relationships we seek are of a different quality from those before. But relating—on whatever level—is what life is about. Perhaps we can relate more freely—which means living more in harmony with ourselves and our fellow human beings.

Question: What is an "act of Grace"? (See page 139.)

Answer: Some event or happening during life that lifts us beyond our ordinary awareness. This can happen when a person comes near to death—as in war or illness. It can arrive through a creative experience or for no particular reason. It can sometimes happen in or after a period of depression. It is the point where the Self for some reason—apparent or otherwise—breaks through.

Question: You speak of the Self—is there a meditation connected to this?

Answer: The aim of the Saturn Meditation is to bring you to a realization of the Self. When you become the god Saturn sitting on his throne looking at yourself, you can begin to experience some detachment over your personal or human nature. As this develops, the point that is the Self starts to grow in strength and awareness. Thus, the more we embrace the positive side of what Saturn has to offer us, the nearer we grow to our own true nature—which is the Self.

Another meditation which can be helpful in respect to the Self is as follows.

After relaxing yourself thoroughly, imagine you are somewhere in the universe surrounded by starry galaxies. Imagine the Lords of Light, Life and Love there, and send your love directly to them—do this for a few minutes. At the end of this time you should have relaxed very deeply. Then imagine your Will is directly linked with Universal Thought; and say from the depths of your heart, "Thy Will Be Done," or, "Not my Will but Thine." Reflect on this thought for several minutes.

Question: What is God?

Answer: If you mean by the word "God" the Supreme Creator of All, then the reply has to be that our finite minds cannot ever truly conceive what God is. That there is a supreme God-head is without doubt.

Question: You seem to believe in reincarnation—what if I cannot believe in it?

Answer: Due to how I work and what I have observed for myself, I feel that reincarnation makes more sense than just one earthly life. But this is my own realization—you must come to your own. Never believe anything just because someone else does. If you are not sure just shelve that problem until one day when you can perhaps look at it and say, "Yes I believe in it," or "No I don't."

Question: Many of the meditation examples given in this book are very descriptive and beautiful, and seem to indicate that the people doing them had some knowledge of the inner workings of the mind, and of spiritual ideals and beliefs. What happens if we have little or no understanding of psychology or esoteric teachings?

Answer: Obviously some of the examples were picked because of their explicit nature. However, most people I work with at the beginning have little if any understanding of how the mind works—and only a rudimentary knowledge of esoteric principles. In this book, I have tried in a simple way to introduce the elements necessary to bring together the esoteric teachings and astrology linked with a simple approach to modern psychology. One man I worked with remarked, after a session in which I read back to him what he said on his Saturn journey, "How beautiful; did I really say that?" Do not doubt what you have within you—for all wisdom is there.

Question: Can I still work with the Saturn energy if I do not understand astrology?

Answer: Yes, of course. Reading this book can open your mind to the many possibilities connected with astrology that you may not have been aware of before. The Saturn Meditation is really very simple, and most people can use it to advantage once they recognize its very simple message—responsibility on the deepest of levels—for oneself and for one's relationships with others.

Appendix II: Tables

Saturn's Positions 1900-2000 A.D.			
Jan. 1, 1900-Jan. 20, 1900	Sagittarius	Nov. 20, 1932-Feb. 13, 1935	Aquarius
Jan. 21, 1900-July 18, 1900	Capricorn	Feb. 14, 1935-April 25, 1937	Pisces
July 19, 1900-Oct. 16, 1900	Sagittarius	April 26, 1937-Oct. 18, 1937	Aries
Oct. 17, 1900-Jan. 19, 1903	Capricorn	Oct. 19, 1937-Jan. 15, 1938	Pisces
Jan. 20, 1903-April 12, 1905	Aquarius	Jan. 16, 1938-July 7, 1939	Aries
April 13, 1905-Aug. 16, 1905	Pisces	July 8, 1939-Sept. 23, 1939	Taurus
Aug. 17, 1905-Jan. 7, 1906	Aquarius	Sept. 24, 1939-Jan. 20, 1940	Aries
Jan. 8, 1906-Mar. 18, 1908	Pisces	Jan. 21, 1940-May 9, 1942	Taurus
Mar. 19, 1908-May 16, 1910	Aries	May 10, 1942-June 21, 1944	Gemini
May 17, 1910-Dec. 14, 1910	Taurus	June 22, 1944-Aug. 3, 1946	Cancer
Dec. 15, 1910-Jan. 19, 1911	Aries	Aug. 4, 1946-Sept. 20, 1948	Leo
Jan. 20, 1911-July 16, 1912	Taurus	Sept. 21, 1948-April 4, 1949	Virgo
July 17, 1912-Nov. 30, 1912	Gemini	April 5, 1949-May 30, 1949	Leo
Dec. 1, 1912-Mar. 25, 1913	Taurus	May 31, 1949-Dec. 31, 1949	Virgo
Mar. 26, 1913-Aug. 24, 1914	Gemini	Jan. 1, 1950-Nov. 21, 1950	Virgo
Aug. 25, 1914-Dec. 6, 1914	Cancer	Nov. 22, 1950-Mar. 7, 1951	Libra
Dec. 7, 1914-May 11, 1915	Gemini	Mar. 8, 1951-Aug. 13, 1951	Virgo
May 12, 1915-Oct. 16, 1916	Cancer	Aug. 14, 1951-Oct. 20, 1953	Libra
Oct. 17, 1916-Dec. 7, 1916	Leo	Oct. 21, 1953-Jan. 10, 1956	Scorpio
Dec. 8, 1916-July 23, 1917	Cancer	Jan. 11, 1956-May 14, 1956	Sagittarius
July 24, 1917-Aug. 11, 1919	Leo	May 15, 1956-Oct. 10, 1956	Scorpio
Aug. 12, 1919-Oct. 7, 1921	Virgo	Oct. 11, 1956-Jan. 5, 1959	Sagittarius
Oct. 8, 1921-Dec. 19, 1923	Libra	Jan. 6, 1959-Jan. 3, 1962	Capricorn
Dec. 20, 1923-April 5, 1924	Scorpio	Jan. 4, 1962-Mar. 23, 1964	Aquarius
April 6, 1924-Sept. 13, 1924	Libra	Mar. 24, 1964-Sept. 15, 1964	Pisces
Sept. 14, 1924-Dec. 2, 1926	Scorpio	Sept. 16, 1964-Dec. 15, 1964	Aquarius
Dec. 3, 1926-Mar. 14, 1929	Sagittarius	Dec. 16, 1964-Mar. 3, 1967	Pisces
Mar. 15, 1929-May 4, 1929	Capricorn	Mar. 4, 1967-April 29, 1969	Aries
May 5, 1929-Nov. 29, 1929	Sagittarius	April 30, 1969-June 18, 1971	Taurus
Nov. 30, 1929-Feb. 23, 1932	Capricorn	June 19, 1971-Jan. 10, 1972	Gemini
Feb. 24, 1932-Aug. 13, 1932	Aquarius	Jan. 11, 1972-Feb. 21, 1972	Taurus
Aug. 14, 1932-Nov. 19, 1932	Capricorn	Feb. 22, 1972-Aug. 1, 1973	Gemini

Saturn's Positions 1900-2000 A.D. (Cont.)

Aug. 2, 1973-Jan. 7, 1974	Cancer	Nov. 18, 1985-Feb. 13, 1988	Sagittarius
Jan. 8, 1974-April 18, 1974	Gemini	Feb. 14, 1988-June 10, 1988	Capricorn
April 19, 1974-Sept. 17, 1975	Cancer	June 11, 1988-Nov. 12, 1988	Sagittarius
Sept. 18, 1975-Jan. 14, 1976	Leo	Nov. 13, 1988-Feb. 6, 1991	Capricorn
Jan. 15, 1976-June 5, 1976	Cancer	Feb. 7, 1991-May 21, 1993	Aquarius
June 6, 1976-Nov. 16, 1977	Leo	May 22, 1993-June 30, 1993	Pisces
Nov. 17, 1977-Jan. 5, 1978	Virgo	July 1, 1993-Jan. 28, 1994	Aquarius
Jan. 6, 1978-July 26, 1978	Leo	Jan. 29, 1994-April 7, 1996	Pisces
July 27, 1978-Sept. 21, 1980	Virgo	April 8, 1996-June 9, 1998	Aries
Sept. 22, 1980-Nov. 29, 1982	Libra	June 10, 1998-Oct. 25, 1998	Taurus
Nov. 30, 1982-May 6, 1983	Scorpio	Oct. 26, 1998-Mar. 1, 1999	Aries
May 7, 1983-Aug. 24, 1983	Libra	Mar. 2, 1999-Dec. 31, 1999	Taurus
Aug. 25, 1983-Nov. 17, 1985	Scorpio		

Pluto's Positions 1900-2000 A.D.

Jan. 1, 1900-Sept. 9, 1912	Gemini	Aug. 19, 1957-April 10, 1958	Virgo
Sept. 10, 1912-Oct. 19, 1912	Cancer	April 11, 1958-June 10, 1958	Leo
Oct. 20, 1912-July 9, 1913	Gemini	June 11, 1958-Oct. 4, 1971	Virgo
July 10, 1913-Dec. 27, 1913	Cancer	Oct. 5, 1971-April 16, 1972	Libra
Dec. 28, 1913-May 26, 1914	Gemini	April 17, 1972-July 29, 1972	Virgo
May 27, 1914-Oct. 6, 1937	Cancer	July 30, 1972-Nov. 5, 1983	Libra
Oct. 7, 1937-Nov. 24, 1937	Leo	Nov. 6, 1983-May 17, 1984	Scorpio
Nov. 25, 1937-Aug. 3, 1938	Cancer	May 18, 1984-Aug. 27, 1984	Libra
Aug. 4, 1938-Feb. 6, 1939	Leo	Aug. 28, 1984-Jan. 16, 1995	Scorpio
Feb. 7, 1939-June 13, 1939	Cancer	Jan. 17, 1995-April 21, 1995	Sagittarius
June 14, 1939-Oct. 19, 1956	Leo	April 22, 1995-Nov. 9, 1995	Scorpio
Oct. 20, 1956-Jan. 14, 1957	Virgo	Nov. 10, 1995-Jan. 25, 2008	Sagittarius
Jan. 15, 1957-Aug. 18, 1957	Leo		

Further Reading

The list below includes most of the works quoted in this volume, and additional material that the reader may find useful.

Assagioli, Alberto. *The Act of Will*. New York: Penguin, 1974.

————. *Psychosynthesis*. New York: Penguin, 1971.

Bailey, Alice A. *Esoteric Astrology*. Albany, NY: Lucis Press Ltd., 1965.

Blake, William. *The Complete Poems,* ed. Alicia Ostriker. London: Penguin, 1977.

Blavatsky, Madame H.P. *The Secret Doctrine*. Pasadena, CA: Theosophical University Press, 1971.

————. *The Voice of the Silence*. Pasadena, CA: Theosophical University Press, 1971, 1989.

Eliot, T.S. *Collected Poems 1909-1962*. London: Faber and Faber Ltd., 1963 and San Diego: Harcourt Brace Jovanovich, 1964.

————. *The Four Quartets*. London: Faber and Faber Ltd., 1979 and San Diego: Harcourt Brace Jovanovich, 1971.

Ferrucci, Piero. *What We May Be*. London: Crucible, 1989.

Fromm, Erich. *The Art of Loving*. New York: Harper Collins, 1956; London: Unwin, 1975.

Greene, Liz. *The Astrology of Fate*. London: Mandala, 1985 and York Beach, ME: Samuel Weiser, 1984.

————. *Saturn: A New Look at an Old Devil*. London: Arkana, 1976 and York Beach, ME: Samuel Weiser, 1990.

Krishna, Gopi. *Kundalini: The Evolutionary Energy in Man*. Boston: Shambhala Publications, 1971.

Leo, Alan. *The Art of Synthesis*. Rochester, VT: Inner Traditions, 1989.

————. *Saturn*. York Beach, ME: Samuel Weiser, 1970.

Maslow, Abraham. *Motivation and Personality*. New York: Harper Collins, 1970.

Rudhyar, Dane. *The Astrological Houses*. Sebastopol, CA: CRCS Publications, 1986.

Sasportas, Howard. *The Twelve Houses*. London: Aquarian Press, 1985.

Steinbrecher, Edwin. *The Inner Guide Meditation*. London: Aquarian Press, 1988 and York Beach, ME: Samuel Weiser, 1988.

Tagore, Rabindraneth. *A Flight of Swans*. London: John Murrey, 1955.

————. *Selected Poems*. London: Penguin Modern Classics, 1989.

Wickes, Frances. *The Inner World of Choice*. Boston: Sigo Press, 1988.

Yram. *Practical Astral Projection*. York Beach, ME: Samuel Weiser, 1972. Pbk 1976.

Resources

1) Books by Madame H. P. Blavatsky may be obtained from your local metaphysical bookstore or you can write to the Theosophical Society's International Headquarters at the following address:

The Theosophical Society
P.O. Box Bin C
Pasadena, CA 91109

2) Visualization tapes of the following are available:

   The Saturn Meditation

   The Pluto Meditation

   The Subpersonality Meditation

For prices and postage, write to Joy Michaud at the following address:

Joy Michaud
The Minster Centre
15 Silver Street
Ilminster
Somerset TA19 ODH
England

3) Bach Remedies—many health food stores now stock the Bach Flower Remedies; those who have no such source are recommended to contact one of the following for both remedies and books:

UNITED STATES
The Ellon Company
P.O. Box 320
Woodmere, NY 11598
Tel. 516 593 2206

UNITED KINGDOM
The Bach Flower Remedies
Unit 6
Suffolk Way
Abingdon
OXON OX14 5JX
ENGLAND
Tel. 0235 550086; Fax 0235 523973

The Bach Centre
Mount Vernon
Sotwell
Wallingford
OXON OX10 OPZ
ENGLAND
Tel. 0491 34678

CANADA
Bach Centre
P.O. Box 4265
Peterborough
Ontario, K9J 7Y8
CANADA
Tel. 705 749 1894

GERMANY/AUSTRIA
Bach Centre German Office
M. Scheffer
Eppendorfer Landstr. 32
200 Hamburg 20, GERMANY
Tel. 040 46 10 41

AUSTRALIA
Martin and Pleasance Ltd.
P.O. Box 2054
Richmond
Vic. 3121
AUSTRALIA
Tel. 427 7422

4) As well as the 38 remedies prepared by Dr. Bach in the 1930's, which are all marketed by the Bach Centre and its distributors, there are the Flower Essence Therapies that have been prepared mostly from North American plant species and have been available to the public since 1978. They are not replacements for Dr. Bach's work, but unique preparations in their own right. They are available from:

Flower Essence Services
P.O. Box 1769
Nevada City, CA 95959
USA
Tel. 916 265 0258

About the Authors

Karen Hilverson, who is a previously published writer of short stories, wrote the chapters entitled "Saturn in Mythology, Literature, and Art" and "Pluto in Mythology, Literature, and Art." She holds a Masters degree from Exeter University, Devon, United Kingdom, teaches English, and is currently working on a novel while residing in her native England.

Joy Michaud is a practicing psychotherapist, hypnotherapist, and astrologer. She gives lectures and holds workshops all over England, uniting her interests in astrology and psychology and demonstrating how people can connect with the mythic images within the unconscious in order to better understand the mind and personality. She is currently working on her next book concerning the influence of Uranus and Neptune on the psyche.

Erich Holmann, the artist of the six black and white illustrations that appear in this book, worked extensively with the Saturn and Pluto meditations before creating this art. His drawings depict much of his own inner journey. Erich's many paintings and drawings are in art collections throughout the world—including those of the Prince of Wales.